LoveNotes. . .

❤

LoveNote. . . In my book, "The Prospering Power of Love," I have described love as not only 'a many splendored thing' but also 'a many splintered thing.' "How to *Really* Love the One You're With" helps the reader to go from the 'splinter' to the 'splendor' of love!

Catherine Ponder, Minister, Author
The Prospering Power of Love

LoveNote. . . People are asking about healthy relationships. How do we create them? What do they feel like? How do I grow from the unhealthy relationships I have been creating into more healthy ones? Here is a book that provides some answers for these questions. The information is timely and relevant. Read and stretch yourself towards learning "How to *Really* Love the One You're With!"

Dr. Bruce Fisher, Ed.D., Author
Rebuilding When Your Relationship Ends

LoveNote. . . Open your heart to the delightful, all inclusive Love in which "we live, and move and have our being." Then follow expectantly, enthusiastically, the gentle steps described by Larry James in his remarkable new book, "How to *Really* Love the One You're With."

J. Sig Paulson
Worldwide Unity Minister/Author/Lecturer

LoveNote. . . "How to *Really* Love the One You're With!" is a profound meditation upon human love in the context of Divine Love; of love as a challenge to know self and learn of the other; of love as a challenge to trust and let go of fear. It will stir you to the very depths of feeling and reflection. It is a wisdom about love which is both fresh and as old as the eternal.

Dr. Larry Losoncy, Ph.D.
Marriage/Family Therapist

LoveNote. . . "How to *Really* Love the One You're With" is a must for anyone in love or searching for love. Larry James presents masterful guidelines that nurture healthy love relationships. His words inspire integrity with compassion. They can help heal the wounded heart.

Anne Boe, Professional Speaker/Author
How to Net Your Playmate (Video) & Is Your 'Net' Working?

LoveNote. . . "How to *Really* Love the One You're With" gently but powerfully lifted me out of the complacency and lethargy I unwittingly let happen in my love relationships. I was deeply touched by this book. It is a 'must read' for everyone on this planet.

> Dr. H. Fred Vogt, Minister Emeritus
> Mile Hi Church of Religious Science

LoveNote. . . If you want self-generating love that's unconditional and stimulates unlimited growth and expansion, read, "How to *Really* Love the One You're With!"

> Mark Victor Hansen, Professional Speaker/Co-Author
> *Chicken Soup for the Soul*

LoveNote. . . Larry James brilliantly shares the "how tos" of having a successful relationship. He has managed to put into words what most of us hide in our hearts.

> Jane Jenkins Herlong
> Professional Speaker/Former Miss South Carolina

LoveNote. . . "How to *Really* Love the One You're With" articulates beautifully the fundamental truth that having a loving relationship with anyone or any aspect of life starts by first loving yourself. As always it's an inside job.

> Richard Imprescia
> Minister of Religious Science

LoveNote. . . "How to *Really* Love the One You're With" is an adventure in self-discovery. Its words are a blueprint for a healthier, happier, extraordinary love relationship with the one you love and with yourself.

> Jack Canfield, Professional Speaker/Co-Author
> *Chicken Soup for the Soul*

LoveNote. . . What a delight it was reading "How to *Really* Love the One You're With!" It is full of wonderful insights and simple reminders that bring us back to love. Thank you for writing a book about love that is loving to the reader.

> Terry McBride, Professional Speaker

LoveNote. . . I have admired Larry James' work for over a decade. Don't miss "How to *Really* Love the One You're With!" It is an informing must-read which will add quality to that treasured relationship in your life!

> Don Hutson, Professional Speaker/Author
> *The Sale*

Also by Larry James

BOOKS:

LoveNotes for Lovers
  Words That Make Music for Two Hearts Dancing!

The First Book of Life$kills!
  10 Ways to Maximize Your Personal and Professional Potential

AUDIO CASSETTES:

Life$kills: The Cassette

A Relationship Enrichment LoveShop™
  *An interactive workshop designed to help you fit the pieces of the
  relationship puzzle together in a healthy way!*

OTHER:

14 Carat Gold Puzzle Pin

How To *Really* Love
The One
You're With!

Affirmative Guidelines For A Healthy Love Relationship

Larry James

How To *Really* Love The One You're With!
Affirmative Guidelines For A Healthy Love Relationship

A Career Assurance Book

Copyright © MCMXCIV ~ Larry James

LoveNotes. . . ™ is a registered trademark of Larry James

This book is designed to provide accurate and authoritative information in regard to the subject matter covered. It is sold with the understanding that the publisher and the author are not engaged in rendering psychological, medical, or other professional services. If expert assistance or counseling is needed, the services of a competent professional should be sought and is recommended.

Printed in the United States of America ~ Third Edition

PUBLISHER'S CATALOGING IN PUBLICATION

James, Larry, 1939-
    How to really love the one you're with! : affirmative guidelines for a healthy love relationship / Larry James
    p. cm.
    Includes bibliographical references.
    Preassigned LCCN: 94-71088
    ISBN 1-881558-02-9

    1. Love. 2. Self-actualization (Psychology) I. Title.

BF575.L8J35   158.'2
                       QB194-507

Cover Design: Jim Weems, Ad Graphics, Tulsa, Oklahoma ~ 800 368-6196

Distribution in the United States and Canada by
LPC Group/Chicago - **800 626-4330**

Published by:

Career Assurance Press
Post Office Box 12695
Scottsdale, AZ 85267-2695
800 725-9223
E-mail: CAPress1@aol.com
WebPage: http://www.adgraf.com/James.html

Contents

Part I
Affirmative Guidelines For a Healthy Love Relationship

Part II
More Reflections on Having a Healthy Love Relationship

Dedication

To the memory of the first woman in my life, my mother, Mary
N. Jarvis.

Her countenance radiated love. Her expressions of unconditional
love for my father, our family, and her countless friends influenced
my life. They ultimately have found further expression in the words
of this book.

LoveNote. . .

Wherever there is love, there is an angel nearby.

~ Karen Goldman

Acknowledgements

♥

My deepest gratitude goes to Dr. Larry Losoncy, Ph.D., without whose guidance, both in therapy and as a friend, this book may never have been written. His counsel is wise and invaluable. He listens.

Words of encouragement and support from my networking friend, Anne Boe, inspired the completion of Part II. Thanks, Anne.

Loving hugs and warm, tender kisses to all the women I have known. I love them all. I have learned invaluable lessons from every one. I believe in Angels.

A special thank you to all of my friends who have shared their many thoughts and feelings about relationships. I cherish their friendship and I love them deeply. Often in small groups and many times in private conversations they - each and every one - shared openly and honestly from the heart. I have learned about relation-ships from many points of view. I warmly appreciate their contri-bution.

I acknowledge and appreciate my sister, Jean Jarvis Pierce, for her unconditional love, support, last minute proofing notes and editorial suggestions. Thanks, Sis!

Thanks to my friends at Novel Idea Book Store for being one of my best sources for books on relationships and more. Bless them. They often took time from their busy schedules to assist me with reference material, tips on good books, literary data and more. I acknowledge their service excellence.

And finally, I humbly acknowledge the Source from which all knowledge flows!

LoveNote. . .

As long as we are looking outside ourselves for intimacy, we will never have it and we will never be able to share it. In order to be intimate with another person, we have to know who we are, what we feel, what we think, what our values are, what is important to us, and what we want. If we do not know these things about ourselves, we can never share them with another person.

~ Anne Wilson Schaef

A Personal Message From the Author...

♥

I wrote this book for me!

My intention was to write guidelines for a healthy love relationship that would assist me in future love relationships. I wrote them with no thought of ever sharing them with anyone but my future love partner and myself.

After telling several close friends what I had written, they requested copies of their own. I was encouraged to publish my thoughts and feelings about relationships.

Part I of this book was first distributed as a limited edition to about two hundred of my special friends and was called, "In Search of a Healthy Love Relationship!" I changed the title to, "How to *Really* Love the One You're With!" for several reasons. After my seminars and keynotes, people who were married would come up to me and say, "You should write a book for us married folks. We are through searching."

It was then I realized that the guidelines I had written for my future love relationship were as valid for people who were already in a committed relationship, married or otherwise, as well as singles in search of, or already in a love relationship.

In addition, the original title I had chosen for *my* book, suggested that to benefit from the book you would need to be in search of a healthy love relationship, not necessarily in one. In retrospect, the original title did little to accurately portray the intent of the book for me either. Since I was completing a relationship when I wrote Part I, the last thing I needed was to get busy searching for a new relationship.

Everything happens for a purpose. I shall forever be grateful for

LoveNote. . .

Lord, grant that I may always desire more than I can accomplish.

~ Michelangelo

LoveNote. . .

The greatest thing a husband or wife can wish for the spouse is spirituality; for soul unfoldment brings out the divine qualities of understanding, patience, thoughfulness, love. Live love yourself, and your goodness will inspire all your loved ones.

~ Paramahansa Yogananda

my former love relationship. I had to experience the pain of a changing relationship to be able to write the words of this book.

The pain of separation found a new, affirmative expression through the words written on these pages. As I wrote, I felt better about the possibilities of future relationships. I spent less time thinking about the hurt and more time focusing on and becoming excited about what might be next for me in the area of relationships.

I began to write what I consider to be some of my most important work up to this point. I was clearly on a mission to define the kind of relationship I wanted. I knew that when I read my book, its affirmative style would help me internalize the information more rapidly; it would become a part of me faster and I could get on with living and loving my life. Perhaps it will have a similar effect on you.

To be sure the words I wrote would lead me in the right direction, I asked my friend and therapist, Dr. Larry Losoncy, to review them for accuracy and authenticity. Only a few new words were added to Part I, otherwise it remains intact since its first writing. Part II is new to this edition.

The introduction that follows was written as part of the original booklet. It sets the pace for the affirmative guidelines in Part I. It is more than an introduction; it is an accumulation of thoughts and feelings that are, in effect, part of the guidelines for a healthy love relationship. You are encouraged not to skim over this section.

I'm proud of the words in this book. I have a personal relationship with them. I have read them hundreds of times. Having an intimate relationship with the words in this book have caused me to have a clearer understanding about what I have to look forward to. These words are now a part of who I am.

While I was writing this book, I also kept a journal. It is interesting now to look back and see how far I've come. Several of the topics found in Part II were created around thoughts and feelings originally expressed in my journal.

In some areas of Part I, the affirmative writing style reflects what I

LoveNote. . .

We cannot really love anybody with whom we never laugh.

~ Agnes Repplier

want as if I already had it. When read in first person, silently or aloud, it is easier to relate to the words.

While I was putting my thoughts on paper, I often would silently question my beliefs about what I had just written. In those moments, I often continued to write in quite another style. I call it a supportive style. In other words, when I began to question, I would gather supportive information to validate the affirmative style.

While the various styles may not necessarily always be anatomically correct from a literary point of view, remember. . . I wrote this one for me as a part of the healing process for my former love relationship. My writing assisted me in being less concerned about being right. Oh, to be happy again!

Some may believe achieving the state of unconditional love to be an impossible dream. I believe that anything is possible when you believe it to be so. For me, I know that unconditional love is a far better path to be on than not. At least when I am clear about what I am aiming for, I know I have a better chance of hitting it.

These words are intended to be guidelines. When put into action . . . together, with your love partner. . . they can serve to keep you both on target.

Unconditional love is the ultimate goal!

My wish is that the guidelines I have chosen for myself may also enrich your love relationships beyond your wildest dreams. May they assist you in really *being* with whoever you choose to be with in a relationship. May they help your relationships to be healthier, more loving, closer, supportive, happier, sexier, more fun to be in and anything else you can think of that you might want in a healthy love relationship!

Celebrate Love!

Larry James
Scottsdale, Arizona

LoveNote. . .

For love does not seek a joy that follows from its effect: its joy is in the effect itself, which is the good of the beloved. Consequently, if my love be pure I do not even have to seek for myself the satisfaction of loving. Love seeks one thing only: the good of the loved.

~ Thomas Merton

Introduction

♥

I have become an astute observer of who I have been in past love relationships. I do not like what I have seen.

Underneath all conflict lies an unforgiving thought. I believe that forgiveness is the key to happiness. Forgiveness is letting go of the past, and is therefore the means of correcting my misperceptions. Perception is a mirror, not a fact.

I have forgiven myself for not being who I needed to be for my former love partners. I now let go of whatever I think my former love partners may have done to me, and what I think I may have done to them. I now release the pain of past relationships. I am now complete with forgiveness in my former relationships.

I am committed to learn from the mistakes of the past, do more of what I have learned from them and to forever commit to intentionally stay focused on what needs to be done in future love relationships on a moment-to-moment basis.

It would never be my intention to drag the stuff of past relationships into a future love relationship. And it is difficult not to. Old habits are difficult to break. I am committed to initiate new behaviors consistent with my desire to grow into a healthy love relationship. I want the kind of love relationship that has each of us exercise responsibility for our individual experience of the other. Not to do so will have the cycle of past mistakes repeat itself. The choices are: be responsible or leave the relationship. I want a love relationship with understanding; one that finds us committed to always be *working together* even when it feels like we don't want to.

Clarity of purpose is now a high priority. I have decided that I can no longer tolerate being unclear about what I want in a healthy love relationship.

LoveNote. . .
___

Tis better to have loved and lost. Than never to have loved at all.

~ Alfred, Lord Tennyson

I have a new intention, that is to use these words as guidelines for reinventing my future love relationship *beginning now!* "How to *Really* Love the One You're With!" is a truthful portrayal of the only kind of love relationship I believe to be worthy of pursuit; one of unconditional love.

Who I am is someone who will always explore new and better ways of *being* in a relationship. I am committed to a love relationship that works for both love partners. Part of the problem in past relationships was that I never clearly defined what I wanted from the relationship nor what I was willing to commit to in the relationship. No longer.

Writing the words in this book has been an adventure in self-discovery. I have learned more about myself than I care to admit. Some discoveries have been painful. I have been excited by others and enlightened by all. Through therapy, meditation and prayer I have been reintroduced to myself. I now know me better and that was an original intention.

I have gone to great lengths to detail some of what I believe makes for a healthy love relationship. Many of the words were inspired by or are from the works of professional therapists skilled in working with couples committed to healthy love relationships. Their books and audio cassette programs have been a godsend.

I am beginning to understand more about what it takes to be related. It takes commitment; a commitment to learn from the lessons that a love relationship presents. If I don't learn the lessons the first time, I know I am destined to relive the same painful experience again and again until the lesson is learned. I am tired of hurting. The payoff for not changing for me has been more pain. This is no longer acceptable. Life has given me a "wake-up" call. This time I am listening.

I am committed to change.

We do what we do perhaps not so much out of habit or because our past experiences make us do it, but because our behavior continues to benefit us, usually by protecting us from something we

LoveNote. . .

Love is a great thing, a good above all others, which alone maketh every burden light.

~ Thomas a Kempis

fear. For most of us, the pain we feel is preferable to the pain we fear. Our fears are a treasury of self-knowledge if we explore them. No amount of thinking about or talking about will get us to the point where we can step out of our fear. *We always have to take the first step while still being afraid.*

With any true inner-growth, the hardest step is always the one you have never taken before. The greater the doubt you step across, the greater the possibility for walking beyond yourself, because doubt and fear form the perimeter of all self-limiting barriers.

When self-discovery becomes more important than being right, then every situation in life presents you with an opportunity to learn about yourself in a new and exciting way. Every time you step past yourself, you win a little more freedom; freedom to take another and yet another step into the great unknown where eventually, with persistence, fear turns into fearlessness.

When we are afraid, we hand over all our power. It doesn't have to be that way. The same mind that created the fear has the same power to redirect our imagination to see and feel ourselves strong and vital; able to overcome every situation. It's our choice! Fear dissipates only as we feel more confident, and confidence grows with successfully meeting the challenge; taking the first step. Fear is a call for help, and therefore, a request for love.

The only effective way to accomplish the change we seek is to understand and overcome the powerful hidden motives that keep us fixed in our present behavior. Jordan and Margaret Paul describes the hidden motive as "intent." Intent is the purpose or the unspoken motivation behind what we do. It is always expressed by our behavior and reacted to by our love partner, though usually invisible to both. We must learn to respect the one intent that dominates our lives and creates most of the difficulties in our relationships; the intent to protect ourselves against any pain, especially disapproval and rejection. Not easy. And I am committed to stay focused on doing whatever it takes!

When my intent is to understand rather than to change my love partner, I can promote her growth, not limit it. Understanding does not necessarily mean agreement.

LoveNote...

Where love is, God is.

~ Unknown

LoveNote...

Love is the master key that opens the gates of happiness.
~ Oliver Wendell Holmes

I have learned that you can have a love relationship with someone you don't understand, *and* that relationship will always be on their terms. *There is a deep commitment within me to learn to shift my focus from solutions to understanding.* Only then can I turn my internal concerns into an adventure in self-discovery.

When I become aware of the cause of the moments pain and how it connects with an emotional response arising from the past, I can then understand the response that is appropriate for me as an adult. I have learned that protecting myself against emotional pain is a pattern learned in childhood, once necessary for survival as a child, but no longer productive behavior as an adult.

Only one response to conflict opens the door to intimacy: an intent to learn from the experience.

I am committed to a life of continuous and never-ending self-examination. I will forever explore the mystery of reality, ever enlarging and refining and redefining my understanding of the world and what is true.

Truth or reality is often avoided when it is painful.

I can reinvent my life only when I have the discipline to overcome that pain. To gain such discipline, I dedicate myself to Truth. The Truth wants what is best for me. The Truth is never further away from me than my wish for its awakening and self-healing insight. Permitting the Truth to do what it is intended to do will permit me to be what I want to be - which is happy!

I hold Truth to be more important, more vital to my self-interest, than my comfort. I consider my personal discomfort relatively unimportant, and, indeed, even welcome it in the service of the search for Truth.

There is a high degree of probability that I may, unintentionally, make some of the same mistakes of the past again. I am human. People occasionally screw up! As I mature and grow in my love relationship, I will, however, make fewer of the same mistakes. I will make new ones. When I do, I will pray for patience from my

LoveNote. . .

Love is a canvas pattern furnished by Nature, and embroidered by imagination.

~ Voltaire

LoveNote. . .

It is never too late to fall in love.

~ Sandy Wilson

love partner, seek forgiveness, learn from the mistake, explore the cause of the error, recommit to do things differently and move on to what's next. I extend the same unconditional love to my love partner when she makes mistakes.

To know how to avoid mistakes or to know how to correct them and not take corrective measures are two of the biggest mistakes I can make.

The dream of a forever love relationship 'made in heaven' or of finding the perfect mate is totally unrealistic. Every man-woman relationship must be worked at, built, rebuilt, and continually refreshed by mutual growth. The goal is not so much in 'getting there;' what is important is to be on the way; loving together; working together; really *being* together; staying together.

The words in this book express my willingness to be healed from the hurts of the past and to begin again in a new and empowering way to experience fully a healthy love relationship.

The affirmative style of defining a healthy love relationship used in this book is powerful. When I read it, it says to me, "This is who I am. This is what I already have." It doesn't mean that I am unrealistic enough to believe that I will not have to do anything differently. I am committed to having a healthy love relationship that works. And I will have to work it. So will my love partner. I am excited to know that the kind of relationship I have defined is possible!

It's true that you become what you think about. I believe this. I know that the more concentrated effort I put into becoming the kind of love partner I choose to be, the more quickly old habits of past relationships will drop away and new habits that complement a healthy love relationship will be established.

I am not actively looking for a love relationship. I am willing to trust that it will happen when it happens. I know that to the degree I am willing to give up my search for a healthy love relationship, I can have it. I know that a natural outcome of letting go will be that I will attract a truly incredible love partner when I least

LoveNote. . .

The gift of intimacy shall be granted when you reach a level of inner-fulfillment which allows for the sharing of one whole individual with another.

~ Karin Owen

LoveNote. . .

Living happily ever after is not the end of a fairy tale. It is the common purpose that all life seeks.

~ Bob Mandel

expect it. I am clear that I do not need any particular woman. *And* I will find whoever finds me.

I intend to stay committed to having these words become a part of who I am. I will stay focused on what I want and who I want to become in my love relationship. I have a deep commitment to stay on the path of self-discovery; to search out new ways of being that support me in being an incredibly great love partner. I will use these words to construct a new me that will attract a love partner with a similar belief system and one who will stand firm on a commitment to do whatever it takes to be in the kind of healthy love relationship that few only dream about.

I acknowledge that the challenge will be to attract a playmate who can similarly subscribe to the same ideals and be true to the commitment to speak the vocabulary of love which is words of love, acceptance, understanding and forgiveness; one who will not run away when the going gets rough; one who will aspire to unconditional love; one who knows all about me and loves me anyway!

How to *Really* Love the One You're With!

Affirmative Guidelines For a Healthy Love Relationship

Part I

❤

LoveNote. . .

The miracle of unconditional love is nurtured by the power of the Divine and our own imagination. _Imagine the possibilities!_

~ Larry James

The Ultimate Goal:
Unconditional Love

I have a love relationship where both love partners have agreement to strive to reach the state of unconditional love; love given with no requirement or expectation of receiving anything in return. It is a love given for the sheer joy of loving, without a payoff from the person who is the object of love.

Lasting enlightenment or true spiritual growth can be achieved only through the persistent exercise of unconditional love. Unconditional love is a healthy choice.

I love myself and my love partner, fully and unconditionally! My love partner loves herself and me, fully and unconditionally!

This is our highest priority.

I know that love is the answer to all questions.

LoveNote. . .

You must love yourself before you love another. By accepting yourself and fully being what you are. . . your simple presence can make others happy.

~ Jane Roberts

LoveNote. . .

All the love in all the tomorrows is in the seeds of love sown today.

~ Larry James

LoveNote. . .

To love yourself is the beginning of a lifelong romance.

~ Oscar Wilde

Self Love

♥

LARRY JAMES

In a healthy love relationship, an inner loving relationship with myself must first be nurtured. I cannot give unconditional love to my love partner if I do not have unconditional love for myself. Self-love and love of others go hand in hand. They are indistinguishable. A healthy love relationship with myself is a high priority. Then, and only then, can I initiate a successful outer love relationship with another.

My relationship with myself is the most important one in my life. Once I have discovered my own commitment to myself, my willingness to be with myself forever, through good times and bad, then, and only then, do I have the foundation to share the commitment with another. Unconditional love of myself creates the space in which to experience spiritual union with my love partner. Not only do people treat me the way I treat myself, I am the one I always have to live with.

I feel loved by my love partner. The sheer joy of finding myself deeply loved is unbelievable and has changed my world, my feelings about life and myself.

The more love I feel, the more love I want to share. I share my love with abandon, lavishly, with my love partner and as a result, experience more love and pleasure from her.

Genuine unconditional love, with all the discipline that it requires, is the only path in this life to substantial joy. When I genuinely love I am extending myself, and when I am extending myself I am growing. The more I love, the longer I love, the larger I become. Genuine unconditional love is self-replenishing. The more I nurture the spiritual growth of my love partner, the more my own spiritual growth is nurtured.

How
To
Really
Love
the
One
You're
With!

LoveNote. . .

If there is no music on the inside, there's no music on the outside.

~ Joe Charbonneau

LoveNote. . .

Love is the most precious gift you can receive. To recognize it when given, you must first experience the gift of giving love to yourself.

~ Larry James

I have a healthy love relationship based upon understanding, acceptance, forgiveness, a willingness to grow and change; one that encourages the intention of encountering ones own fear, and one that supports a conscious decision to act in loving ways to my love partner. I know that what you place your attention on grows stronger.

I know that if I want my love relationship to fulfill its purpose, I must enlighten my experience of it. I must drop judgements, preconceived notions, opinions, positions and beliefs about it.

When I do this, a miracle occurs. The miracle that occurs is that the love relationship I have becomes the love relationship I want; the one that nurtures and supports me; the one that truly empowers me.

**How
To
Really
Love
the
One
You're
With!**

LoveNote. . .

Until one is committed, there is hesitancy, the chance to draw back, always ineffectiveness, concerning all acts of initiative (and creative). There is one elementary truth, the ignorance of which kills countless ideas and splendid plans: that the moment one definitely commits oneself, then Providence moves too. All sorts of things occur to help one that would never otherwise have occurred. A whole stream of events issues from the decision, raising in one's favor all manner of unforeseen incidents and meetings and material assistance, which no man could have dreamt would have come his way.

~ W. H. Murray

LoveNote. . .

Love never fails.

~ I Corinthians 13:8

Commitment

♥

I have a love relationship with total commitment; deep commitment; a commitment to each other to always do whatever it takes to create a trusting, loving and healthy love relationship. Commitment is the foundation, the bedrock of my unconditional love relationship.

My love partner and I are totally committed to each other's happiness and we consistently demonstrate our love in many ways. I know that I can only foster personal and spiritual growth of my love partner through a love relationship of constancy.

Commitment is a deep trust, a devotion discovered in the choice to be together. Commitment needs no agreements because it is based on desire, not obligation.

Commitment in a love relationship also means commitment to the process of mutual understanding and forgiveness, no matter how many conversations it takes, nor how uncomfortable those conversations might sometimes be.

A forever love relationship requires devotion, loyalty and a mature ability to commit.

Commitment in my love relationship means the kind of commitment that demands that all of our skills in the area of loving each other, compassion, understanding, acceptance, release, forgiveness and selflessness are pushed to the limit. The cure for selfishness is more love, from within.

My love partner and I share a mutual commitment to consistently create and sustain a vibrant, deeply rewarding love relationship.

9

How
To
Really
Love
the
One
You're
With!

LoveNote. . .

To forgive is the highest, most beautiful form of love. In return, you will receive untold peace and happiness.
~ Robert Muller

LoveNote. . .

If we really want to love, we must learn how to forgive.
~ Mother Teresa

LoveNote. . .

Love is an act of endless forgiveness.
~ Peter Ustinov

LoveNote. . .

Genuine forgiveness is participation, reunion overcoming the powers of estrangement. . . We cannot love unless we have accepted forgiveness, and the deeper our experience of forgiveness is, the greater is our love.
~ Paul Tillich

LoveNote. . .

One pardons to the degree that one loves.
~ Francois De La Rochefoucauld

Forgiveness

Forgiveness is the key to happiness in a love relationship. It ends the illusion of separation, and its power can change misery into happiness in an instant. Forgiveness means choosing to let go, move on, and favor the positive.

The first step in the forgiveness formula is for me to release my hurt and anger safely and constructively, without dumping on my partner. The second step is the acknowledgement that both of us can grow from the incident. I am not afraid to admit how I might have contributed to any miscommunication and upset. The issue is not to blame or find fault, but to learn and grow. The third step must include the expression of love, trust, and intimacy. The more I can express my feelings of tenderness and commitment, the more easily my partner can acknowledge my pain.

Forgiveness is not complicated. It is simple. I simply identify the situation to be forgiven and ask myself, "Am I willing to waste my energy further on this matter?" If the answer is "no," then that's it. All is forgiven. Telling someone is a bonus. Choice is always present in forgiveness. You do not have to forgive *and* there are consequences.

When I feel forgiveness is necessary, I do not forgive for my *love partner's* sake. I do it for *me*, not for her. She does not *need* to be forgiven. She did what she did and that is it - except for the consequences, which my love partner must live with.

Forgiveness releases my love partner from my criticism and also releases me from being imprisoned by my own negative judgements. Every time I forgive, I am radiating Divine Love from the living center of myself and directing It to the one forgiven.

11

**How
To
Really
Love
the
One
You're
With!**

LoveNote...

To love and be loved is to feel the sun from both sides.
~ David Viscott

LoveNote...

The ideal love relationship is the coming together of two imperfect persons who are drawn together because each has the potential and the will and the commitment to become a blessing of growth for each other.
~ Eric Butterworth

LoveNote...

No one has ever loved anyone the way everyone wants to be loved.

~ Elbert Hubbard

Acceptance

♥

I have a relationship that is healthy in that both of us accept that each has unique thoughts, feelings, interests, and viewpoints and that we do not feel threatened by differences, because we trust, respect, and honor each other. True acceptance of our own and each other's individuality and separateness is the only foundation upon which a mature, healthy relationship can be based and from which unconditional love can grow.

Differences may be more of a reason for a good love relationship than evidence of incompatibility. I believe that the more I resist accepting my love partner as she is, the more her traits will persist in annoying me.

Within my love relationship is an abiding commitment for each love partner to be their own person; two whole people, complete in themselves; each loving themselves and loving each other, unconditionally. I believe that in a mature adult relationship, one's individuality is not lost, but nurtured. Each partner experiences freedom, independence, and integrity.

Wholeness comes mainly from within. Two halves make two halves; two whole, loving love partners can create a truly incredible love relationship. In my healthy love relationship I take joy in my partner's growth and respect her individuality.

The more freely my love partner and I feel to express our individuality, the more satisfaction we get; the more passion and joy we experience with each other.

We learn from each other. We do not concern ourselves to decide whose beliefs and values are "right," but rather to

13

**How
To
Really
Love
the
One
You're
With!**

LoveNote...

Speak only words of love. The vocabulary of love are words of acceptance and understanding.

~ Larry James

LoveNote...

Peace of mind occurs when we put all our attention into giving and have no desire to get anything from, or to change, another person.

~ Gerald G. Jampolsky, M.D.

LoveNote...

Be not angry that you cannot make others as you wish them to be, since you cannot make yourself as you wish to be.

~ Thomas A. Kempis

understand and respect the reasons each of us have for believing as we do.

I have a love relationship that strives for a partnership of
equals, each person responsible for their own health and
happiness, loved and each encouraged by the other. Unconditional love allows each partner to unfold in their own
way. I know the more self-sufficient I can be, the less pressure I put on the relationship.

Three important steps in a healthy love relationship are do
not judge, do not rationalize and do not defend your point
of view.

When I stop judging, interpreting, evaluating, analyzing,
labeling, defining and describing, in the silence of non-judge-
ment, spontaneously there is healing and room for an effective love relationship to mature.

One of the most important things I can do in my relationship is to lose the need to defend my point of view. This
does not mean that I do not have a point of view; it means
only that I am not attached to rigidly defending it. I fully
understand that life within a healthy love relationship is the
co-existence of many points of view.

The mechanics of perception are such that no two people
are going to experience a given reality in exactly the same
way. I know that a deep loving connection occurs only between my love partner and me when we are not defensive;
when we are not threatened by each other's feelings; when
we can flow together without feeling overwhelmed by the
other.

I will not try to change my love partner because the more I
try to change her, the more likely she is to feel rejected and
unloved, and therefore resistant to change. I need and have
the same commitment from her. I believe that only when
both partners are striving to be full and complete within
themselves can love and happiness blossom. Change will
only come when my love partner or I desire it.

LoveNote. . .

Lending support to your love partner is not standing behind them, it's holding hands and walking beside them . . . all the way.

~ Larry James

LoveNote. . .

Love is the free exercise of choice. Two people love each other only when they are quite capable of living without each other but *choose* to live with each other.

~ M. Scott Peck

Support

♥

I know that to have an intimate love relationship, my love partner and I both need to feel the freedom to live our lives in ways that satisfy each of us individually and still meet each other's needs.

I always do all I can to help my love partner grow to her optimum potentiality and capacity, even if that means she must sometimes be away from me and do things without me. I am always seeking to discover and support what inspires my love partner.

The purpose and function of my love partner is to grow personally and spiritually and to be the most of which she is capable, not for my benefit but for her own. Because of my unconditional love for her I want her to become all that she is capable of becoming.

I want the best for my love partner and will never feel threatened by her successes in any way. My love partner is unique and I love her for who she is, not for what I may expect her to be. My love for her is given without strings - no "ifs" or "buts." I encourage emotional self-sufficiency in my love partner. I believe that the need for individual autonomy is not only compatible with a successful forever relationship, but can be a strong contributor.

**How
To
Really
Love
the
One
You're
With!**

LoveNote. . .

A good marriage is that in which each appoints the other guardian of his solitude. Once the realization is accepted that even between the closest human beings infinite distances continue to exist, a wonderful living side by side can grow up, if they succeed in loving the distance between them which makes it possible for each to see the other whole against a wide sky.

~ Rainer Maria Rilke

LoveNote. . .

Love from one being to another can only be that two solitudes come nearer, recognize and protect and comfort each other.

~ Han Suyin

LoveNote. . .

Don't smother each other. No one can grow in the shade.

~ Leo Buscaglia

Creating Space

♥

LARRY JAMES

Someone said that it is possible to be together so much that we suffocate each other. Perhaps. I do not allow this to happen in my love relationship. I believe that love includes letting go when my partner needs freedom; holding her close when she needs care. I am committed to creating space in my relationship when needed.

We have learned to cherish both intimacy and solitude. We never feel tied to each other.

At the heart of love, there is a simple secret: the lover lets the beloved be free. My love partner and I require different mixes of independence and mutuality, and the mix is freely discussed and renegotiated from time to time when necessary.

When two people in a love relationship are complete within themselves they do not experience the love they have for others as diminishing, detracting, or threatening to the love they share. They are secure within the relationship.

Insecurities bring forth jealousy, which, in effect, is a cry for more love. It is within your rights to ask for more affection when self-doubts surface, however, the indirect way that jealousy asks for it is counterproductive. Excessive possessiveness is inappropriate. Jealousy is the surest way to drive away the very person you may fear losing.

It is an irony that the more possessive I am, the more love I demand, the less I receive; while the more freedom I give, the less I demand, the more love I receive. I take great pleasure in watching my love partner be fully free and fully alive!

We encourage each other to widen our circle of friends.

LoveNote. . .

Love is not possessive.

~ I Corinthians 13:4

LoveNote. . .

To limit the scope of our love to just a few people is to constrict our identity and imprison ourselves.

~ Robert Perry

LoveNote. . .

But let there be spaces in your togetherness, and let the winds of the heavens dance between you. Love one another, but make not a bond of love: let it rather be a moving sea between the shores of your souls. Fill each other's cup but drink not from one cup. Sing and dance together and be joyous, but let each one of you be alone. Give your hearts, but not into each other's keeping. For only the hand of Life can contain your hearts. And stand together yet not too near together; for the oak tree and the cypress grow not in each other's shadow.

~ Kahlil Gibran

We each seek to ever expand our horizons. We enjoy celebrating life together and with friends!

I know that if I expect to be the only person who matters to my love partner I am setting myself up for disappointment. As wonderful as true love can be, no one person can meet all your needs. My love partner is, and will always be my very best friend, and she is not my only friend.

I fully expect my love partner to have other passionate interests other than me. To extend the freedom to develop her own interests in other people and hobbies can only empower our relationship. Freedom can never confine. It can never be detrimental to the relationship. It can only open up many exciting and previously undiscovered opportunities to enjoy life.

When my lover is pursuing areas in which she excels, she is happy. I enjoy her most when she is happy. People are easier to love when they are happy.

Trust is forever present in our love relationship; trust and deep commitment to each other, loyalty and devotion. This allows us the freedom to care about people of the opposite sex and to enjoy friendships with them, and when we sit down together in the evening to share the events of the day, we do not have to ask if our love partner has been faithful.

The stronger and more secure we become, the more we are willing to be ourselves while encouraging our love partner to do the same.

Genuine unconditional love not only respects the individuality of the other but actually seeks to cultivate it, even at the risk of separation or loss. The ultimate goal remains the spiritual growth of my love partner, the solitary journey to peaks that can be climbed only alone.

I believe that no matter how committed my forever love relationship, I will always be "single" as well as a part of a couple. Unconditional love is a special, intense connection, and it is not an answer to all or even most individual problems. No one can make me happy but me.

LoveNote...

Immature love says: "I love you because I need you."
Mature love says: "I need you because I love you."

~ Erich Fromm

LoveNote...

Don't brood. Get on with living and loving. You don't have forever.

~ Leo Buscaglia

People Need People

♥

LARRY JAMES

I have discovered that *need is not a dirty word*. For a long time I felt that "need" was dependence. I have learned the difference. Need and dependency are not the same thing. I was afraid that I would give up my power if I said that I needed you. Needing others is not a mistake. Giving up your responsibility for satisfying *your* needs is a mistake.

You *need* others and you *depend* on yourself.

To paraphrase author, Michael Lynberg, our need to stand alone must be tempered by our need to stand together. And paradoxically, our independence must be tempered by our dependence.

Having needs goes hand in hand with being fully human. Acknowledging our needs gives purpose to our relationship.

Everyone has a need to be needed, which often becomes confused with love itself. As long as you have someone dependent on you, you may feel like a useful human being, with something to offer.

I let go of this need! And letting go of this need usually brings up my own needs, which I may have been denying by attending to others.

I know that I do not need other people to make me happy. When I learn to be happy with myself, I am in the perfect place to attract a love partner who can be happy alone. Two people who can be happy alone can be twice as happy together!

LoveNote...

Marriage is not a static state between two unchanging people. Marriage is a psychological and spiritual journey that begins in the ecstasy of attraction, meanders through a rocky stretch of self-discovery, and culminates in the creation of an intimate, joyful, lifelong union.

~ Harville Hendrix

LoveNote...

The entire sum of existence is the magic of being needed by just one person.

~ Vi Putnam

I have learned that *the problem is not that you need love, but that you depend on others to create love in your life.* I must depend on myself to create a healthy love relationship.

I need you in my life because you help me feel a sense of belonging. I need someone to care about and someone who cares about me. I need someone to love unconditionally and someone who will love me unconditionally. I need your encouragement. I need to encourage. *I need you!*

I need love in my life. I need you as my love partner in my life *and* I will never depend on you to create my happiness for me. Only I can do that. Therefore, I am responsible for fulfilling all of my needs.

This new understanding eliminates the fear that, if I say I need you, I am giving my power away to you, and that I will be hurt if you do not fulfill me. I do need you, and if you do not fulfill my basic needs, I am responsible for finding someone else who will. I am thankful for this new awareness.

Whether or not I realize the full potential of a forever love relationship does not depend on my ability to attract the ever elusive perfect mate for there is no such thing. It depends on my willingness to seek knowledge of the parts of myself that I have long since buried. I have an eagerness to do something to facilitate personal changes in my behavior.

I forgive myself for not being perfect and stop expecting superhuman feats from myself. Any aim for perfection is a moving target. Indeed, I accept myself as I am instead of what I think I should be.

LARRY JAMES

25

How
To
Really
Love
the
One
You're
With!

LoveNote. . .

Responsibility in a healthy love relationship is the willingness to be the author of all your experiences, and to never disown authorship of the self-created experiences that you call bad or unpleasant. Bad experiences are an invention of the mind to avoid responsibility.

~ Larry James

LoveNote. . .

I am free and responsible for all that I do, for all my acts, for all my commitments. Freedom and responsibility are one. And only then is it I who do it. A free man is responsible, and my freedom lies in the assumption of that responsibility.

~ William Ofman

LoveNote. . .

Even if marriages are made in heaven, man has to be responsible for the maintenance.

~ John Graham

LoveNote. . .

The problem will be solved when I accept that happiness is a present attitude, not a future condition.

~ Hugh Prather

Responsibility

♥

LARRY JAMES

I have a love partner who agrees to share equally in the responsibility for what transpires between us in the relationship; one who shares in the idea that it takes two to tangle; one who knows a love crisis is a challenge to mobilize the best in ourselves and grow; one who acknowledges "problems" as potential "opportunities" we co-create.

When you are out standing in a storm, do not blame the storm!

As we each come to understand our equal share in creating problems. . . blame, self-doubt, and discord give way to personal responsibility, accountability, mutual respect, and intimacy.

In a healthy love relationship, things are easiest when both love partners take responsibility for the whole, not just their halves.

My love partner and I are not responsible for the feelings of each other. We can only be responsible for how we feel, not for how each other feels in reaction to what we do. The converse is also true: we are responsible for our own feelings and reactions about what the other love partner does.

LoveNote. . .

Your happiness should never be subject to any outside influence.

~ Paramahansa Yogananda

LoveNote. . .

Happiness ensues; it cannot be pursued.

~ Victor Frank

LoveNote. . .

Don't worry. Be happy.

~ Bobby McFarrin

LoveNote. . .

The door to happiness swings outward.

~ Soren Kierkegaard

Be Happy!

♥

LARRY JAMES

Problems in our love relationship do not have to make us unhappy!

Unhappiness is a choice! I can only make myself miserable, and *I cannot make myself happy!* Unhappiness does not come at me, it comes from me. The desperate search for happiness is the continuation of unhappiness.

Unhappy feelings are born out of my love relationship failing to conform to my ideas of what I think I need to be happy. Letting go of what I think I need to be happy is the same as letting go of my unhappiness.

Happiness is never driven to look for itself. It is itself. Authentic happiness is a natural state. Therefore, to experience unhappiness, you must allow unhappiness to happen.

Happiness is a present attitude, not a future condition. It is the natural expression of a stress-free life. It is a part of life to be found within living. Real happiness then, is effortless and happiness is also a choice!

In the past I believed that the reason for my unhappiness was because someone or something outside of me was making me feel that way. This simply is not true. I am responsible for my own happiness!

How
To
Really
Love
the
One
You're
With!

LoveNote. . .

In the all-important world of family relations, there are other words almost as powerful as the famous "I love you." They are "Maybe you're right."

~ Oren Arnold

LoveNote. . .

The secret of a successful marriage is to treat all disasters as incidents and none of the incidents as disasters.

~ Harold Nicholson

LoveNote. . .

It's not the conflict, but what we do in the face of conflict that leads either to difficulties and distance or to freedom and intimacy.

~ Jordan and Margaret Paul

Setbacks Are Natural to Progress

♥

LARRY JAMES

Life will always have its share of difficulties, in the midst of which I can choose to be satisfied and loving. Plateaus and setbacks are natural to progress. Growth in an intimate relationship is never in a straight, upward line.

When disputes occur, we aim for a resolution in which we both win, where we both can be right, and, as much as possible, both get our needs fulfilled.

Do we want to be happy or right?

We always look for the cause of the problem to find the solution. We see through the unhappy condition to its *actual* cause. We let the problem reveal its true nature to us. Only a look at the real problem can reveal the *real* solution. However problems may appear at first, they are almost never what we initially think them to be. Finding the solution involves a change in perception, since the solution must have existed all along, right there within the problem.

To willingly confront a problem early, before we are forced to confront it by circumstances, means to put aside something pleasant or less painful for something more painful. It is choosing to suffer now in the hope of future gratification rather than choosing to continue present gratification in the hope that future suffering will not be necessary.

Problems do not go away. They must be worked through or else they remain, forever a barrier to the growth and development of the human spirit.

True love means sticking it out and solving problems that arise rather than running away. Trials and tribulations are to make, not break us. Those things that hurt, instruct. Love becomes a deeper experience of unity amid diversity.

LoveNote. . .

Lord, when we are wrong, make us willing to change, and when we are right, make us easy to live with.

~ Peter Marshall

LoveNote. . .

To love means never to be afraid of the windstorms of life. Should you shield the canyons from the windstorms you would never see the true beauty of their carvings.

~ Elizabeth Kubler Ross

LoveNote. . .

Genuine love is volitional rather than emotional. The person who truly loves does so because of a decision to love. This person has made a commitment to be loving whether or not the loving feeling is present.

~ M. Scott Peck

A commitment of this kind requires a willingness to risk being hurt and rejected, and yes, at times, even feeling un-loved.

Love partners must regularly, routinely and predictably, attend to each other and their love relationship no matter how they feel. The person who truly loves does so because of a decision to love. They have made a commitment to be loving whether or not the loving feeling is present. If it is, so much the better; but if it isn't, the commitment to love, the will to love, still stands and is still exercised.

I believe that a problem or crisis only becomes a breaking point when we fail to use it as a turning point in our relationship.

**How
To
Really
Love
the
One
You're
With!**

LoveNote...

Seldom or never does a marriage develop into an individual relationship smoothly and without crises. There is no birth of consciousness without pain.

~ C. G. Jung

LoveNote...

Before you can *get* anything different from this life, you must first *do* something different. Before you can *do* anything different with your life, you must first *know* something different. Before you can *know* anything different, you must first suspect and then confirm that it is your present level of understanding that has brought you what you now wish you could change.

~ Guy Finley

Learn From Your Mistakes

LARRY JAMES

♥

I am the architect of my own discomfort.

Realizing mistakes I make are avenues through which I can expand my awareness, my knowledge and understanding, I am willing to learn from them whatever I can. I do so gratefully.

All personal difficulties are born out of a lack of understanding. If we will place learning before our pleasure, one day learning will come before our pain. As we awaken to see things as they really are, our pains disappear. Real pleasure is not the *opposite* of pain, it is the *absence* of it.

When we avoid the legitimate suffering that results from dealing with problems, we also avoid the growth that problems demand from us. The secret is to never wallow in the suffering any longer than is necessary to learn the lesson the suffering presents.

I see upsets not only as an exterior circumstance to be remedied, but as an interior condition to be understood.

Mutual loving confrontation is a significant part of all successful and meaningful healthy love relationships. Without it the relationship is either unsuccessful or shallow.

Confrontation is always preceded by careful and scrupulous self-examination of the worth of our wisdom and motives behind the need to confront. It is always done with a loving respect for our love partner's own path in life and with a responsibility to exercise loving leadership when we feel our lover appears to need such leadership.

**How
To
Really
Love
the
One
You're
With!**

LoveNote...

Our marriage used to suffer from arguments that were too short. Now we argue long enough to find out what the argument is about.

~ Hugh Prather

LoveNote...

A marriage is like a long trip in a tiny row boat; if one passenger starts to rock the boat, the other has to steady it; otherwise, they will go to the bottom together.

~ David Reuben

I always trust that my love partner loves me, even when her actions may indicate otherwise. Love assumes at all times that my partner is lovable and loving is her essence, and that any negative behavior, such as threats or sulks, is a response to pain and frustration and is a challenge to me to further understanding.

LARRY JAMES

LoveNote. . .

We are healed of a suffering only by experiencing it to the full.

~ Marcel Proust

LoveNote. . .

Your heart is not living until it has experienced pain. . . The pain of love breaks open the heart, even if it is as hard as a rock.

~ Hazrat Inayat Khan

Healing the Hurt

♥

LARRY JAMES

I believe that when a couple makes a decision to create a more satisfying relationship, they enter a stage of transformation, and love becomes infused with consciousness and will. Ultimately it takes a lifetime together for a couple to identify and heal the majority of their childhood wounds.

The psychological importance of working through painful resentments cannot be underestimated. When old patterns are broken, a whole new world of possibility is born. Not to release and rise above suppressed feelings of hurt and anger is to remain imprisoned by them.

Fulfillment in my current love relationship depends on successfully healing and learning from past hurts. Unless I am willing to do so, similar conflicts may appear in the future. I open up to pain. Opening to pain is the only way I have to learn what it has to teach me. When I shut out pain, I shut out awareness. To experience love more deeply I must be vulnerable to hurt.

I do not feel the need to exit a good relationship simply because my love partner has restimulated painful memories of past love relationships. I can focus on healing my unresolved hurts and strive for a mature love relationship that becomes a healthy and emotionally supportive experience.

In a healthy love relationship there is always movement - at times toward intimacy, at other times toward withdrawal and distance.

I am secure in my love relationship and never panic during a difficult phase of withdrawal. I unconditionally love my

**How
To
Really
Love
the
One
You're
With!**

LoveNote. . .

When I am hurting, I ask my lover for a hug. There is divine healing in a silent, close embrace.

~ Larry James

LoveNote. . .

Recovery means claiming your circumstances instead of your circumstances claiming your happiness.

~ The Grief Recovery Handbook

LoveNote. . .

You don't need to leave a good relationship simply because your partner has restimulated painful memories or your old emotional tapes. To the contrary, you can heal your unresolved hurts and have an adult love relationship that becomes a corrective emotional experience.

~ Harold H. Bloomfield, M.D.

partner and remember my commitment to do whatever it takes to encourage the experience of balance in the love relationship.

I am seldom upset for the reason I think I am. I am aware that upsets go much deeper than present circumstances may indicate. There may be an innate tendency for me to repeat my childhood dramas. I can and will work through them.

What I need is an understanding of how my upbringing affected me, what negative attitudes I may have internalized, and how to change these outdated emotional habits.

I need to trust you and be loving in spite of the past. I need to trust you and love you because of the past.

I will continue to examine the past for evidence of how I was denied adequate nurturing and how I repressed essential parts of my being. I will do this through therapy, prayer, meditation and reflection, and by becoming a more astute observer of everyday events.

**How
To
Really
Love
the
One
You're
With!**

LoveNote. . .

Be watchful, stand firm in your faith, be courageous, be strong. Let all that you do be done in love.

~ I Corinthians 16:13-14

LoveNote. . .

Problems call forth our courage and our wisdom; indeed, they create our courage and our wisdom. It is only because of problems that we grow mentally and spiritually.

~ M. Scott Peck

Share Your Thoughts and Feelings

❤

I will no longer assume that my love partner can read my mind.

When love partners share their thoughts and feelings with each other, we need to listen with understanding and compassion, knowing that this sharing is a sacred trust. There is no value in suffering in silence.

Daily I renew my commitment to my love partner, deliberately doing things that give her pleasure, and creating a safe and nurturing environment. I will add to this, safety and validation by learning to communicate openly and effectively.

I understand that a forever, committed relationship cannot happen easily, or automatically, without defining what it is that I want, without asking, and without reciprocating.

I will go against my instinct to focus on my own needs and make a conscious choice to focus on hers.

I live each day with her as if it were my last.

**How
To
Really
Love
the
One
You're
With!**

LoveNote. . .

The gem cannot be polished without friction, nor man perfected without trials.

~ Chinese Proverb

Say "No" to the Past

LARRY JAMES

♥

I have a relationship that is based on mutual caring and love, the kind of love that can be best described by the Greek word "agape." Agape is a self-transcending love that redirects Eros, the life force, away from myself and toward my partner in an intentional act of healing; it focuses my energy on healing my partner.

It is when I direct my energy away from myself and toward my partner that deep-level psychological and spiritual healing begins to take place. In healing my partner, I am slowly reclaiming parts of my own lost self.

As we both work toward this aim, the pain of the past is slowly erased, and both of us experience the reality of our essential wholeness. We must stop expecting the outside world to take care of us and begin to accept responsibility for our own healing.

Our unconditional love supports us in being strong enough to survive hurt which is an inevitable part of every love relationship. When we gather the courage to search for the truth of our being and the truth of our partner's being, we begin a journey of psychological and spiritual healing.

Whenever I perceive that the past is following me, I stop, turn around, stand firmly and face it! I no longer allow what happened to me in former relationships to rob me of the exciting possibilities the future holds for me and my love partner.

The energy you use to hold on to the past is the same energy you need to create your future. The extent to which you cling to the past is the extent to which you are blocked

LoveNote. . .

I have always felt sorry for people afraid of feeling, of sentimentality, who are unable to weep with their whole heart. Because those who do not know how to weep do not know how to laugh either.

~ Golda Meir

LoveNote. . .

I believe that the reason of life is for each of us simply to grow in love.

~ Count Leo Tolstoy

in receiving what you truly want in a relationship. If you don't believe you deserve a healthy love relationship, you will never create it.

When you make peace with your past, you can get on with your future.

I know that unhealed wounds casts a shadow that stands between those desiring an unconditional love relationship. If people are going to be healed, they have to change. Doing things differently is frightening. It always was and always will be. It always requires courage and involves risk.

While it is often true that what one partner needs the most, the other partner may be least able to give, it also happens to be the precise area where that partner needs to grow. The love that we send out to each other is touching and healing our own wounds. We cannot worry about having ups and downs; they are a sign that we are healing.

Crying is a natural release. Tears are a gift from God. They may be God's way of allowing others to know you are sharing how you feel as truth of the heart, not of the head.

My love partner allows me to see through to her heart when she lets me see her tears. Often I cry tears of joy and tears of sadness. I am thankful for this God-given release.

How
To
Really
Love
the
One
You're
With!

LoveNote...

The only way to have a friend is to be one.

~ Ralph Waldo Emerson

Friends and *Lovers*

❤

**LARRY
JAMES**

I am learning to see my love partner without distortion; to value her as highly as I value myself; to give without expecting anything in return; to commit myself fully to her welfare. Only then can love move freely between us without apparent effort. It's unconditional love between best friends.

When we are able to love in this selfless manner, we experience a release of energy. We cease to be consumed by the details of our relationship, or the need to operate within the artificial structure of exercises; we spontaneously treat each other with love and respect. Love becomes automatic.

My forever lover is my very best friend!

I believe that friendship among lovers is essential to unconditional love and is the primary ingredient for a deep and lasting love relationship. I trust her with the deepest murmurings of my soul. She knows the best and the worst of me and yet loves me through and through; a friend as well as a lover.

**How
To
Really
Love
the
One
You're
With!**

LoveNote. . .

To go beyond yourself is to cause yourself to stretch; to put fear aside; to step outside of the box you live in, to slam the door and to consciously decide to stay there.

~ Larry James

Going Beyond Yourself

♥

LARRY JAMES

I am learning how to overcome my limitations and develop my capacity to love, not because I expect love in return, but simply because my love partner deserves to be loved.

The greatest rewards of living and loving come when I step out of the bounds of my ordinary existence and extend myself beyond what I believe my limits to be. I am willing to give myself to the relationship, and to be willing to be what grows out of it.

I have a love partner who is supportive of us making key choices together, fully listening to and learning from what each love partner has to say.

Love is embracing differences and discovering ways in which to build a common life-style, share decision-making, and take equal responsibility for the results.

I know the only legitimate power I have in my relationship is to inform my partner of my needs and to change my own behavior to better meet my love partner's needs. If I feel my lover taking me for granted, it is always and only my responsibility to request the love and appreciation I deserve.

While it may be true that a certain amount of compromise is necessary for a love relationship to endure, I do not want a love partner who will do 'anything' for me.

I want a lover who will, when necessary, draw the line beyond which she will not go and who will openly communicate her feelings to me. I want a love partner who has allegiance to a higher power rather than to my own unpredict-

How
To
Really
Love
the
One
You're
With!

LoveNote...

There is no difficulty that enough love will not conquer.
~ Emmet Fox

able and often fickle perceptions of reality that show up in my weaker moments.

I consistently continue to stretch beyond resisting what I fear and move into more positive, nurturing behaviors for my love partner. I have a relationship that is a self-sustaining vehicle for personal and spiritual growth; one that supports and encourages a positive climate for consistent change; one that offers patience, understanding and forgiveness when errors are made.

How
To
Really
Love
the
One
You're
With!

LoveNote. . .

Never close your lips to those to whom you have opened your heart.

~ Charles Dickens

Really Talk to Each Other

LARRY JAMES

In order to experience the kind of relationship I want, I accept the fact that, in order to understand each other, my love partner and I must have clearly developed channels of communication. I cultivate transparency of myself by being a master in the art of self-disclosure. I know that when the inclination to reveal myself to the one I love is blocked, I close myself to her and experience emotional difficulties. I promise to never hide behind a facade.

I will forever practice telling my love partner exactly what pleases me, decreasing her reliance on mental telepathy. I express preferences instead of demands. I believe that I can never know myself except as an outcome of disclosing myself to her.

In ways I may not fully understand, self-disclosure helps me to see things, feel things, imagine things, hope for things that I could never have thought possible. The invitation to transparency, then, is really an invitation to authenticity. It is also an invitation to allow myself to be vulnerable.

When I allow my love partner to see me for who I really am right now, I am less afraid I will be rejected in the future. When my love partner accepts and loves me unconditionally, I know I will never have to hide in the relationship in the future.

To have inner peace it is necessary to be consistently loving in what I think, in what I say and in what I do. I think thoughts of love. I speak words of love. I demonstrate unconditional love for my love partner in all that I do.

Openness means being willing to communicate my deepest

LoveNote. . .

I remember the many times you held me close and whispered, "I love you." and the many times you said nothing; just smiled and I got the same message.

~ Larry James

LoveNote. . .

The people we are in a relationship with are always a mirror, reflecting our own beliefs, and simultaneously we are mirrors reflecting their beliefs. So relationship is one of the most powerful tools for growth... if we look honestly at our relationships we can see so much about how we have created them.

~ Shakti Gawain

feelings. There can be no intimacy without conversation. The only way my love partner and I can truly communicate is to tell the truth. Truthful communication moves love partners and creates a condition of unity, love and satisfaction.

For intimacy to grow in a healthy love relationship there can be no withholding; feelings - both positive and negative - must be shared equally between love partners. The act of withholding the truth is always potentially a lie.

The energy required for the self-discipline of honesty is far less than the energy required for withholding. My love partner and I are dedicated to the truth and live in the open, and through the exercise of our courage to live in the open, we become free from fear. Fear cannot exist whenever insight is valued above feeling frightened.

I listen when my lover shares without making judgements. My heart is always open to hear what my love partner has to say.

How
To
Really
Love
the
One
You're
With!

LoveNote. . .

Today I could have been satisfied to only hold you for a moment. Yes, *to only hold you;* for a quiet, loving moment!

~ Larry James

Time Together

♥

LARRY JAMES

My love partner and I regularly schedule leisurely breaks for intimate conversation. There is always plenty to discuss when my love partner and I get together in the evening. Sometimes it's across the table with a cup of specially blended coffee, facing each other with our hands touching to see what a difference "undivided attention" makes.

We often talk freely about our feelings, for we both experience hundreds of different emotions during the day. We silently pause for a deep look. Far down into each others souls we look. Rich, rewarding conversation is possible when we seek it. This special time together allows us to begin each new day with no shadows of the past.

Self-exposure demands some risk of being hurt. Courage is called for. When we are open and vulnerable together, we have made an intimate connection. In an atmosphere of acceptance, I can gradually bare the most sensitive areas of my soul.

I am open to share my innermost secret thoughts and feelings with her. Being open and getting to know and be known by my lover is exciting and emotionally enriching.

Heart-to-heart communication requires an emotional atmosphere of caring, safety, and trust. Fear inhibits love. Fear, however, cannot exist in the presence of love. My integrity dictates a willingness to risk having my weaknesses and imperfections seen by my partner. A healthy love relationship allows two people to fully know each other and still love each other!

As love partners we place great importance on being avail-

How
To
Really
Love
the
One
You're
With!

LoveNote. . .

It's the heart afraid of breaking that never learns to dance.
~ From the song, "The Rose"

LoveNote. . .

In the relation of a man and a woman who love each other with passion and imagination and tenderness, there is something of inestimable value, to be ignorant of which is a great misfortune to any human being.
~ Bertrand Russell

able to each other; on practicing the togetherness of accomplishing a shared task like cooking a meal together or surprising our love partner by making the meal ourself; doing work together, instead of her doing the dishes and me washing the car, we work together to wash the dishes then wash the car together.

Why not do both tasks together and enjoy the company of each other in the process?

We make grocery shopping a weekly event. We find mutual pleasure in being in each other's presence and accomplishing a task together.

Birthdays, anniversaries and holidays are days that call for celebration. We cherish these special moments together.

Tender moments of togetherness are necessary for a love relationship to grow. They must be tempered with the balance that the benefits of separateness also promote. Balance between closeness and separateness must be respected.

**How
To
Really
Love
the
One
You're
With!**

LoveNote...

The first duty of love is to listen.

~ Paul Tillich

LoveNote...

The road to the heart is the ear.

~ Voltaire

Listen!

♥

The principal form that the work of unconditional love takes is attention. When I love someone I give them my attention; I attend to their personal and spiritual growth. When I love myself, I attend to my own personal and spiritual growth.

By far the most common and important way in which I can exercise my attention is by listening.

My love partner is a person of great value and worthy of my attention. Listening to my love partner is an act of love.

I promise to always cultivate my ability to listen to my love partner. I believe that it is unreasonable, and a breach of trust, for me to deny my lover's report of her feelings, thoughts, and expectations. Intently listening invites my love partner to share what is in her soul.

I listen with my eyes and ears. Listening with my eyes shuts out all other interests for the moment. I cannot truly listen to her and do anything else at the same time. I am always interested in her innermost thoughts and feelings. I hang on her every word.

True listening, total concentration on my love partner, is always a manifestation of love. An essential part of true listening is the discipline of temporarily giving up or setting aside of my own prejudices, frames of reference and desires so as to experience as far as possible my love partner's world from the inside; hearing what is truly from her heart. This kind of listening is unconditional love in action.

Genuinely attending to my lover assures a deepening of our

LoveNote. . .

Your love partner must be your best friend as well as your lover. Between best friends there should be no secrets even when there are no words.

~ Larry James

love relationship. I never argue with her feelings. I am always receptive, without interrupting or jumping to conclusions, so that she feels listened to and can freely share. I am a student of my love partner, consistently discovering what makes her tick and what makes her ticked.

I always remember that more often than not, when my love partner wants to talk, she only wants someone to listen and not to dispense advice.

I respect the mystery of my love partner; accepting that I will never understand her completely.

I dare never break a confidence with my love partner. I trust her with my secrets and she trusts me with hers.

**How
To
Really
Love
the
One
You're
With!**

LoveNote. . .

Indifference is like water to a fire. The flame of love grows dim with indifference to your love partner's needs.
~ Larry James

LoveNote. . .

Every good lover I've ever known has developed a finely tuned sensitivity to others, and is regularly, atentively, aggressively noticing what makes his or her mate happy.
~ Alan Loy McGinnis

LoveNote. . .

What you take for granted disappears!
~ Larry James

Placing Value on Needs

♥

I accept the limited nature of my own perceptions and become more receptive to the truth of my partner's perceptions. As a result, we experience a whole new world opening up to both of us.

I value my love partner's needs and wishes as highly as I value my own. I am learning new techniques to satisfy my basic needs and desires. I am becoming more aware of my drive to be loving and whole and united with the universe. I accept the challenges of creating a lasting love relationship.

I resist having expectations for what I think my love partner *should* do for me. Ours is a love relationship without 'shoulds.' I am grateful for all that she contributes to the relationship.

Our deep love for each other has us sharing equally in the duties and responsibilities of being a couple. I acknowledge my love partner for all of the things she does for me, both great and small.

I am committed to never take my playmate for granted.

**How
To
Really
Love
the
One
You're
With!**

LoveNote...

Affection can withstand very severe storms of vigor, but not a long polar frost of indifference.

~ Sir Walter Scott

LoveNote...

If you and your love partner always agree, one of you may be unnecessary.

~ Larry James

Handling Anger

♥

LARRY JAMES

I have a love partner that has a clear understanding that loving each other and living together often guarantees some hurt, anger and frustration. I am learning that underneath the anger is hurt and underneath the hurt is love. Caring makes one vulnerable.

I view our disagreements as a signal that my love partner needs care and understanding from me.

I promise to give my love partner the gift of hearing her anger without becoming defensive. I know that the more I resist listening when my love partner is angry, the more she will persist in giving me what I do not want to hear. Because she is angry does not mean I am not loved. I know you can love and be angry at the same time.

To be angry is to suffer. Anger hurts most whoever is angry. I am sensitive to how my anger is expressed. I stop and think before I speak. I promise to only express my anger to get it out, not to win. In a healthy love relationship, expressions of anger are always followed by expressions of love.

When I have a need to communicate my hurt or desire for a specific change, I understand that sometimes disagreements can occur.

My love partner and I view arguments as constructive. A good argument; one that does not seek to make my love partner wrong and make me right; one that searches for understanding; one that releases tension and facilitates an emotional breakthrough, can help our relationship evolve to a new level of love and understanding.

69

How
To
Really
Love
the
One
You're
With!

LoveNote. . .

Never to be angry, never to disagree at all seems to most of us a sign not of love but of indifference.

~ Allan Fromme

Love allows room for disagreements, mistakes, and sadness. I always apologize when I am wrong. It is not a sign of weakness; it is a sign of strength. A crisis in my love relationship allows transformation of a potentially destructive problem into a challenging opportunity for intense communication, greater commitment, more mutual respect, more passion, and ultimately, deeper love.

Perfection is not necessary. Real love begins when I am able to see the flaws and weaknesses in my love partner and love her anyway. I will always seek to understand why my love partner feels the way she does. I will learn to appreciate and respect my love partner's different point of view.

When it comes to feelings, no one is wrong.

**How
To
Really
Love
the
One
You're
With!**

LoveNote. . .

Affection as the essential principle of relatedness is of
the greatest importance in all relationships in the world.
For the union of heaven and earth is the origin of the
whole of nature. Among human beings likewise, spontaneous affection is the all-inclusive principle of union.

~ I Ching

Affection

I have a love partner who openly communicates affection and commitment. There is little more that turns me on than knowing that my love partner loves and cares for me and is unafraid to tell me. My love partner has an extraordinary ability to silently communicate with her eyes the depth of love she has for me in her heart. I like not only to be loved, but also to be told that I am loved.

I promise to always openly speak of my affection and love for my love partner. I love her and have no care of who knows it!

A kiss, a hug, a touch are important moments in which love partners share intimacy. These moments of affection signify careful attention and a special awareness to your lover's innermost wants and needs. They give your future together more of a chance.

It is important to have someone to love and to put aside any hesitancy to display affection at times other than when you want something.

I believe that love is also something you do. Love is as love does. I am never content with only telling my love partner that I love her; I promise to show it in expressions of affection.

Love is an act of will, both an intention and an action. It is something you *do* as well as something you *feel*.

I have a love relationship where the romance continues; where both partners continue to do things that they considered romantic when the love relationship began.

How
To
Really
Love
the
One
You're
With!

LoveNote. . .

Speak to me with your eyes. Whisper words I cannot hear and I will know your heart has spoken. You have touched me with your love. I will respond in kind.

~ Larry James

Examples might be: sending a very special love card; surprising her with flowers; experiencing the emotional closeness holding hands can bring; an unexpected, warm, passionate kiss; celebrating special days together in special ways; planning "for no reason" surprises; calling the office of your love partner for a fifteen second "I love you!" call; taking a canoe trip together; hiring a caterer for a special candlelight dinner at home, around the fireplace complete with fresh flowers on the table; sitting together on a blanket in the park looking for four-leaf clovers; giving unexpected gifts for no other reason except to express love; telephoning thoughtful love messages to your lover's answering machine; extending an invitation to take a shower together, even when you don't need one; bringing each other breakfast in bed or going out for a special breakfast together; proposing a toast to your lover in the presence of close friends; writing your love partner an erotic love letter; taking a hand-in-hand walk together; enjoying a hide-away weekend together far from telephones and TV and in general doing extraordinary things for each other in a caring, loving way.

As healthy love partners we instinctively switch roles from time to time. It adds spice and variety to our relationship. It is also a process that diminishes our mutual dependency. A healthy love relationship can exist only between two strong and independent people!

We consistently do all we can to make our love relationship exciting. We know the consequences of becoming negligent in planning for the continuation of the conditions that brought us together in the first place. We devote whatever time and energy is necessary to create the conditions for ecstasy in our relationship.

We share the magic of the moments about how our love was born. We relive our special moments of intimacy in private conversations and pledge to keep alive the simple pleasures that keep the fire burning between us. We plan to have fun together. We are spontaneously affectionate.

How
To
Really
Love
the
One
You're
With!

LoveNote. . .

You've been in love; you know what it's like. It's a sense of delight, not just in the person you love, but in all people, in yourself, in life. Suddenly you see beauty, excitement everywhere. You're not afraid to express your love; passionately, gently, in words, or in silence. And you feel strong, generous and fully alive.

~ George Weinberg

LoveNote. . .

Want the romance to continue? Treat your lover as a mystery. What if you didn't know who she really was, just like when you first met. That kind of not knowing. For the romance to continue you must look for and create ways to keep the magic of love alive! Love her for who she is, not for who you think she is or who you think she should be.

~ Larry James

We share our innermost thoughts and feelings. We withhold nothing, for to do so closes down the possibility for the openness we both desire and need for intimacy to thrive in our relationship.

These special moments become a powerful aphrodisiac, in that, to continue to know each other better in this manner, reminds us of the intense conversations we had when we were first together; falling in love; staying up all night, talking and touching.

We are committed to have the romance continue!

LoveNote. . .

Activity together moves love to another level. When energy flows, love grows.

~ Larry James

LoveNote. . .

Love is the secret key; it opens the door of the Divine. Laugh, love, be active, dance, sing, become a hollow bamboo and let this song flow through you.

~ Bhagwan Shree Rajneesh

LoveNote. . .

(It is) far better to keep our lives lighted with hope, alive with creative activity, and open to the fresh air of worthwhile ideals.

~ Michael Lynberg

Planned Activities

♥

I engage in several high-energy, fun activities each week with my love partner. These activities might include bicycling, exercising together, walking, tennis, hot-air ballooning, sky diving, roller skating, swimming and then lounging with the one I love in the hot tub, horseback riding, high energy lovemaking, hiking or skiing or anything thing else that we agree might be fun.

I am learning that physical fitness allows for the full pleasure of being alive and loving others. I have tapped into the self-improvement habit; body, intellect, emotional skills, relationships, and spirit! Radiant health is a reflection of the experience of joy and love. I am willing to learn to do new and exciting things that put me with the one I love.

I have dropped the idea that I have to complain when things push me to my limits. I instead concentrate on the good for my body and my relationship that can come from fun activities. I am a commitment to have fun with the one I love *and I will have fun in my life!*

I lower my resistance to change in the activity area by repeating the new behavior often enough so that it feels familiar and therefore safe.

I am healthy and vibrantly alive! I have love on my side. Love is the most powerful energy in the universe because Love is God. I call forth energy and actively pursue vigorous activity, and in so doing, demonstrate unconditional love for myself and my love partner!

I believe when I have exuberant fun with my love partner we identify each other as a source of pleasure and safety, which intensifies our emotional bond.

LoveNote...

Love grows, oh, so slowly when nursed only by complaints.

~ Larry James

Love Note...

Love doesn't make the world go 'round. Love is what makes the ride worthwhile.

~ F. P. Jones

LoveNote...

A balance of excitement and quiet pleasures allows a relationship to grow.

~ Harold H. Bloomfield, M.D.

We register a positive flow of energy. We know that the activity that triggered it is connected to life and safety, and we begin to connect with each other on a deeper, unconscious level.

The couple that plays together, stays together.

My partner and I take turns creating an adventure day or weekend outing that is memorable and exciting for both of us. We look for creative ways to have fun to keep the magic of love alive.

I pledge to do whatever it takes.

LoveNote. . .

Satisfying sexual contact contributes significantly to making a relationship successful. Pleasure is inherent in sexual experiences, and moments of shared physical intimacy, in which two people pleasure one another to fulfillment, can provide a foundation for a relationship that can withstand potentially destructive external pressures. Sexual behavior can convey passion, intimacy, love, and tenderness. Though words may enhance, the vitality and depth of feeling of the communication is expressed through immediate sensory experience. The touches, smells, sounds, and sights of lovemaking are profound communications. Lovemaking is a natural and poignant human experience that no one should be needlessly denied.

~ Leslie Cameron-Bandler

Making Love

♥

Great sex is an active ingredient in our love relationship.
Sex is fun and pleasure is good for us. Pleasure is God's
love in our bodies. Making love is surrendering to a higher
form of energy than any one love partner can experience
alone. Making love is two love partners experiencing their
oneness with each other.

When we make love, we are much greater than the sum of
our parts. It is spiritual as well as physical. We never forget the spiritual source of our love. Making love is a Divine idea. *We never allow making love to become the supreme expression of the absence of God in our lives.*

Sex gives us an enormous opportunity to exercise responsibility. I believe that the sexual experience is immeasurably
heightened when both love partners feel free to mutually
share their likes and dislikes, cares and concerns and hon-
ors each other for their choices.

My love partner is the consummate lover. She openly dis-
closes her sexuality; free of inhibitions. I also invite my
love partner to know me intimately. Making love with one
another elevates us to a level of satisfaction for which there
are no words.

Sex is the ultimate expression of the joy of life; of being
together. It is a Divine connection. Our oneness has a
spirituality that transcends the physical. My lover and I
enjoy a slow buildup of sexual energy and cosmic union,
not a quick orgasm. We are in this together. I respond to
her every desire. Pleasuring her pleasures me.

The highest form of pleasure comes when you give yourself

**How
To
Really
Love
the
One
You're
With!**

LoveNote. . .

I would find myself a lonely man if I have memories of you and our passionate moments of making love and no one to share them with but myself.

~ Larry James

LoveNote. . .

To love is to find pleasure in the happiness of the person loved.

~ Baron Gottfried Wilhelm von Leibnitz

LoveNote. . .

It is not easy to find happiness in ourselves, and it is not possible to find it elsewhere.

~ Agnes Repplier

LoveNote. . .

Trust blazes new trails. It creates the opening for intimacy to exist. Among lovers, trust invites the spark of the Divine to ignite their passion. "Hold me."

~ Larry James

fully with love, creating a mystical ecstasy that allows both love partners to be lost in time and space, if only for a few brief moments.

My love partner and I both know that our individual sexual fulfillment is primarily up to each other, not our love partner. Our love making is a beautiful expression of love at its most Divine level of happiness; a demonstration of reverence for God's ultimate gift of Love to us as lovers.

Intimate love partners share playfulness. I have a love partner who is playful when we make love. Sexual playfulness is vital for continuing to experience each other as lovers. We both feel free to be ourselves. Ours is a maturing sexual love relationship, and as lovers we discover an even greater source of sexual excitement by revealing our emotional selves and communicating heart-to-heart in our sexual play.

In the passion of making love, my playmate and I communicate a profundity of love that words cannot carry. Being together in this fully present and intimate way opens the channel of communication to allow for full disclosure of emotions and the expression of our innermost desires.

We never allow our love making to be a routine act of fulfilling desire. To do so would invite boredom. Intimate love is an adventure of shared warmth and spontaneity. We have spontaneity in our lovemaking; knowing that spontaneity among lovers must always be balanced with kindness, care, and respect for each other.

We occasionally have our very own private party in the bedroom or anywhere else our imagination takes us that might stimulate and excite us. We allow our imagination and creativity free rein.

To keep the magic alive, on occasion, we reenact the night we first made love. A perfect fit! We do not expect our love relationship to be exciting without making it exciting.

**How
To
Really
Love
the
One
You're
With!**

LoveNote. . .

Love today, right now, without condition or requirement. Live each day by love. Seize love when it comes your way and as quickly, give it away. Celebrate love!

~ Larry James

LoveNote. . .

I can think of nothing that excites me more than watching you become lost for the moment in the heat of our passion.

~ Larry James

LoveNote. . .

Touch me! Love me gently with your touch. When it is a genuine expression of true love, touch can bring you intimately closer to another human being than can thousands of words.

~ Larry James

LoveNote. . .

There is one temple in the universe - the human body. We touch heaven when we touch the human body.

~ Thomas Carlyle

The intimate and trusting atmosphere we create together allows an occasional flirting with mutually acceptable fantasies; a powerful stimulus to sexual pleasure. Anything goes as long as love prevails: touch, tongue, tickle; silk, satin, lace; the kitchen table, the patio in the moonlight, the hot tub or Bennigan's parking lot.

Making love is an open window of discovery; an exciting adventure of each other; allowing exploration of a depth of passion attainable to only the few.

I feel a little closer to heaven each morning when I awake to the kiss of my own very special angel.

My love partner and I work together to make our love sanctuary more beautiful and comfortable to enliven and make special our intimacy.

A balance of excitement and quiet pleasures allows a relationship to maximize its potential. My love partner and I have a deep need for the gentleness of a passionate kiss, tenderness, caressing, fondling, and touching each other.

We experience touch as an expression of caring, of comforting and of expressing warm affection. Touching enlivens our lives. It nurtures our love relationship. The gift of touch contains within it the miracle of healing and bonding. Touch is a means of connecting emotionally, physically and spiritually. The gentleness of touch communicates, "I love you," and is not always a prelude to passion.

Our physical nakedness reflects our emotional honesty, and our intimate physical embrace denotes our emotional acceptance of each other. Physical intimacy is the goal of our sexual expression. With intimacy comes a deeper level of exposure of one's self, a profound feeling of enrichment of us joining as one and loving acceptance by each other.

Foreplay is often found in the quietness of loving words.

**How
To
Really
Love
the
One
You're
With!**

LoveNote. . .

Love is like sitting with my back to the fireplace. I can feel the warmth without ever seeing the fire.

~ Ed

LoveNote. . .

Last night I made love with an angel. She was so hot her eyes danced as if to escape the fire of our passion.

~ Larry James

LoveNote. . .

My love partner and I have and enjoy ever-increasing love, health, happiness, wealth, wisdom, harmony, full self-expression, luxurious living spaces, easy and plea-surable travels and sexual bliss.

~ Bob Mandel

LoveNote. . .

There is no such thing as too much intimacy.

~ Paul Pearsall, Ph.D.

In an atmosphere of safety and trust, we derive much pleasure from giving a full-body massage and receiving one, never neglecting any part of our bodies. The deliberate, slow motion of massage stirs passion and builds desire. It allows us to tune in to our lover's innermost feelings.

Candlelight, soft music, a glass of wine, fragrant oils, a soft feather, a vibrator or two and more are all a sacred part of this Divine ritual. We use our imagination and enjoy one another. We savor the magic of the moment. Massage is communicating with sensitivity what we find most pleasurable and erotic; it is making love with our fingers.

I use my mind and body to demonstrate love and warmth. I cherish every new encounter of my lover's touch.

My lover's body is a temple, the container of my loved one's soul. I honor it. I respect it. I encourage her to whisper what pleasures her.

We listen for the sensual sounds our music makes. We know our lover's body like a musician knows his instrument and we play it for all it's worth. We make beautiful music together. She often assists me in writing the score. We take turns leading the orchestra. Our love making is a symphony of supersex. Fully expressing our feelings in this way lessens pressure and anxiety, increases love and deepens trust. We continue to rediscover the things that give us pleasure and bring feelings of closeness.

Sex that is deeply enjoyed is freely given and taken, with deep soul-shaking climaxes, and makes each love partner become humble at the remembrance of joys past and expectant of those yet to be discovered and enjoyed. I am attracted to the majesty of sexual union with my love partner and excited by the promise of its lofty secrets.

I am becoming a master at being passionately intimate with the one I love. Sparks fly! We can feel the sexual electricity in the air when we are together. We tingle when we

How
To
Really
Love
the
One
You're
With!

LoveNote. . .

Erotic love, if it is love, has one premise. That I love from the essence of my being - and experience the other person in the essence of his or her being.

~ Eric Fromm

LoveNote. . .

Chains do not hold a marriage together. It is threads, hundreds of tiny threads which sew people together through the years. That is what makes a marriage last - more than passion or even sex.

~ Simone Signoret

LoveNote. . .

I invite the divine warmth of my graceful angel to embrace me with tranquility and peace. Her passionate, peaceful qualities gently touch my heart. Her soothing presence bathes me with her radiating love. I acknowledge her for the divine idea she is.

~ Larry James

LoveNote. . .

Passion is pure energy, aliveness, and like life itself, it starts off neutral; it is a given. We are the ones that give the energy of passion direction and meaning. The more we have succeeded in channeling passion into love, the more attractive we have become to each other, and the more attractive our relationship has become to both of us.

~ Henry James Borys

mingle. Whatever my lover and I find ourselves doing in the flow of making love is right and beautiful.

We share our passion without fear, and with patience, commitment, and trust. This level of emotional sharing generates a limitless flow of sexual energy. I seek not just sensory gratification but Divine union with my lover.

My love partner is someone who shares my desire to devour life for the romantic adventures that make life delicious.

LoveNote. . .

The real relatedness between two people is experienced in the small tasks they do together; the quiet conversation when the day's upheavals are at rest, the soft word of understanding, the daily companionship, the encouragement offered in a difficult moment, the small gift when least expected, the spontaneous gesture of love.

~ Robert A. Johnson

LoveNote. . .

A successful marriage requires falling in love many times, always with the same person.

~ Mignon McLaughlin

Really Be *Together*

♥

LARRY JAMES

My love partner and I share a mutual commitment to hold aside no less than one evening each week, a purposely scheduled event, where we can be alone together; an evening that is sacred in that we allow nothing to disrupt our coming together as two very best friends and lovers.

This special evening is only for the two of us. It is an opportunity for us to become reacquainted with each other week to week. It is a time that allows us to begin to know each other with a greater depth of understanding. It is a time of cozy conversation and touching. It is our time to say, "I care about you! I love you!" It is a time of romantic celebration!

We never take our special evening for granted.

I consistently work at being a great love partner, and as I gain a more realistic view of my love relationship, I realize that a forever love relationship requires commitment, discipline, and the courage to grow and change.

Creating a lasting friendship takes time and energy. Creating a forever relationship takes committed love, a lot of understanding, consistent effort and much work.

LoveNote. . .

We can never know love if we try to draw others to ourselves; nor can we find it by centering our love in them. For love is infinite; it is never ours to create. We can only channel it from its source in infinity to all whom we meet.

~ J. Donald Walters

LoveNote. . .

Your confidence in living rests in believing that God's love is all that you are.

~ Renette Schmidt

LoveNote. . .

The aim of all spiritual practice is love.

~ Sai Baba

LoveNote. . .

And if you desire to have this intent (to reach God) summarized in one word, take but a little word of one syllable. And such a word is LOVE - and fasten this word to your heart so it may never go away no matter what befalls you. And if any thought presses on you to ask what you would have, answer with just this one word.

~ The Cloud of Unknowing

LoveNote. . .

Gratitude to God becomes the way in which He is remembered, for love cannot be far behind a grateful heart and thankful mind.

~ A Course in Miracles

LoveNote. . .

God is perfect love. There is only one Presence and one Power in our lives, God the Good, Omnipotent.

~ Unknown

The Third Love Partner

♥

LARRY JAMES

My love partner and I share similar spiritual values. Higher spiritual values give meaning and purpose to our relationship. They determine what we will turn away from and what we will move toward. Shared spiritual ideas are the basis for a lasting, fulfilling love relationship.

We put our trust and faith in each other *and* in our inner Source; a Higher Power.

I celebrate the God that gave me you.

When concern for each other's spiritual evolution is absent, dependency flourishes because dependent people are only interested in their own nourishment.

In the case of unconditional love the aim is always spiritual growth.

Unconditional love implies commitment and the exercise of wisdom.

When we are concerned for our love partner's spiritual growth, we know that a lack of commitment is likely to be harmful and that commitment to that love partner is necessary for us to manifest our concern effectively. A shared concern for the other love partner's spiritual growth, in a sense, diminishes mutual dependency.

LoveNote. . .

And above all these things put on love, which binds everything together in perfect harmony.

~ Colossians 3:14

LoveNote. . .

Love is the law of God. You live that you may learn to love. You love that you may learn to live. No other lesson is required of man.

~ Mikhail Naimy

LoveNote. . .

If you want to be loved, be lovable.

~ Ovid

Higher Communication

♥

LARRY JAMES

I continue to pursue the truth about how to transform a forever love relationship into a more conscious, growth-producing partnership. Intimacy, the most profound of interpersonal human pleasures, grows in an atmosphere of peace.

Prayer and meditation open the heart. With higher communication comes a peace that passes understanding. It increases our capacity for love and enjoyment. Anxiety, tension, and irritability are reduced; doubts and insecurities fade.

Peace of mind is the goal.

When relaxation and quiet pleasure are the basic bond in a love relationship, the likelihood of deepening love and emotional rewards is great. Prayer and meditation contributes to mental clarity, lasting emotional ease and allows me to see my love partner anew.

The more frequent our dialogues with God, the greater our chance of coming upon truths we can genuinely call our own.

I am committed to this spiritual discipline and know it will support me in having my truly incredible relationship endure.

When we nurture ourselves and others on a spiritual path of unconditional love without a concern of 'what's in it for us', we become more lovable. Love finds us.

The love we express for each other nurtures us. So it is with Divine love.

LoveNote...

Love is not the plaything of human volition but the action of Divine law.

~ Charles Fillmore

LoveNote...

If you would learn the secret of right relations, look only for the Divine in people and things, and leave all the rest to God.

~ J. Allen Boone

Let Love Be Your Guide

♥

LARRY JAMES

Love is guiding me. Every moment, every day, I take advantage of the opportunity to express more and more love. That which I love in others, I am. I first express love toward myself, to my love partner and everyone I meet. As God loves me, so I love myself, fully and unconditionally. I have unlimited love to give.

Without love I cannot fully live. I must have love to survive, and I do not have to have love from a particular person. If I get stuck thinking that I do, there is one person in the world whom I cannot have love me: it is the person I think I need.

I am thankful for love, the love that God has centered in my soul and which flows over the threads of my thoughts into the world where I live and love. Love binds me to the whole of Creation and makes me one with all there is. I thank God for unconditional love in my relationships, for I know God is Love and Love indwells my being.

I believe that there is a Divine power that goes before me and makes perfect my way. I no longer look to the past to help guide me to a secure future.

I no longer ask how; I step fearlessly into the spiritual now. When I am uncertain, I go ahead and step forward anyway. My decision in favor of this bold new action thrusts me into the present where the actual moment itself teaches me everything I need to know about how to proceed. This action places me under the guiding influences of an Intelligence that never fears the unknown because its very nature is understanding.

LoveNote. . .

Yea, though I walk through the valley of the shadow of death, I will fear no evil for Thou art with me.

~ Psalms 23:4

LoveNote. . .

Divine love is perfect peace and joy.

~ William Law

The reward, after I take the first step, is the sweet and relief-filled discovery that who I am cannot fail.

Truth will take care of me; it will never lead me to an impasse. The Truth itself promises that only good can come to me.

How
To
Really
Love
the
One
You're
With!

LoveNote...

It takes no strength to let go.

~ Guy Findley

Letting Go

♥

LARRY JAMES

I am willing to trust. I know that to the degree I am willing to give up my search for a healthy love relationship, I can have it. I know I can have whatever I am ready and willing to receive. Individual receptivity is everything. Without it, nothing changes. With it, all things are possible. I no longer insist upon *my* choice.

I know that the only thing I lose when I let go of something I am afraid to live without is the fear itself. I am stronger than anything that frightens me!

I let go of the past, and I am free to think clearly and positively in the present. I am not my past.

Letting go is the natural release which always follows the realization that holding on is an energy drain and it hurts. Letting go happens effortlessly when there is no other choice. Letting go does not mean giving up.

Letting go is a journey that never ends. Never. It only begins - over and over again - each time I can glimpse something higher than my own painful certainty over who I think I am. There is always something higher; a life beyond the limits of my present sight.

To see what is further I must be willing to lift my eyes from their present point of focus. Release always follows revelation and real revelation is always a glimpse of something that was only just out of sight.

I know that stress in my love relationship exists because I insist! What I resist, persists. I am tied to whatever I avoid.

**How
To
Really
Love
the
One
You're
With!**

LoveNote...

A life without love in it is like a heap of ashes upon a deserted hearth - with the fire dead, the laughter stilled, and the light extinguished.

~ Frank P. Tebbetts

LoveNote...

The heart loves, but moods have no loyalty. Moods should be heard but never danced to.

~ Hugh Prather

It is a mistaken belief that I must push my love relationship in the direction I choose that keeps me in a strained and unhappy relationship with it. Reality has its own effortless course, and I can either embrace its way or struggle end-lessly with mine.

I do not need power to flow.

I let go of that part of myself that is certain it is better to suffer and feel like someone than it is to just let go and qui-etly be no one. I give birth to a new me that never has to hold on to anything because it is *already everything.*

I dare to walk away from all of the familiar but useless mental and emotional relationships that give me a temporary but unsatisfactory sense of self. My true identity is calling me and to hear it I must be willing to endure, for as long as necessary, the fear of self-uncertainty.

This form of seeming self-abandonment eventually turns into my greatest pleasure as it becomes increasingly evi-dent that the only thing certain about fear is that it will *always* compromise me. When it comes to who I really am, there is no compromise.

Let go of the past. The past is yesterday. It is irretrievable. When you relate to the past, you relate to no one or any thing. You are literally talking to yourself. No one else is listening. You have already heard all you have to say about that, so, let go.

A Course in Miracles says, "You cannot really *not* let go what has already gone. It must be, therefore, that you are maintaining the illusion that it has not gone because you think it serves some purpose that you want fulfilled."

It is certifiable insanity to conjure up your own reality based on the past and relate to it, rather than to relate to the present which is the only reality.

**How
To
Really
Love
the
One
You're
With!**

LoveNote. . .

Relationships are part of a vast plan for our enlightenment, the Holy Spirit's blueprint by which each individual soul is led to greater awareness and expanded love. Relationships are the Holy Spirit's laboratories in which he brings together people who have the maximal opportunity for mutual growth.

~ Marianne Williamson

LoveNote. . .

He that loveth not knoweth not God; for God is Love.

~ I John 4:8

I say goodbye to the past and hello to the present.

I am enthusiastic about who I am becoming! I know that no one sincerely asks for a new life until they are thoroughly dissatisfied with the old one. I am *and* I let go. When I allow myself to let go of what is old, I stay true to what is new.

I believe that as with all insight, higher understanding itself contains not only the instructions I must follow, but the strength I will need to carry them out.

Starting life over again is the key to a new me. I see the beauty and significance of starting over - over and over and over. Every present moment is always new and new is always *right now!* The new dies to the ever-new in an endless celebration of Life.

This is it!

I live in the present. I never let the past dictate the direction of the present moment. I give my best to my endeavors.

What lies ahead for me can only be good.

True peace and harmony are a part of who I am.

I have come to the realization that what is possible for me to become only truly changes when I am willing to see what is impossible for me to continue being.

My true nature is already fully independent and flying freely. I have found my wings.

I let go and let God. And so it is.

Thank you, Father!

How to *Really* Love the One You're With!

More Reflections on Having a Healthy Love Relationship

Part II

How
To
Really
Love
the
One
You're
With!

LoveNote. . .

The heart is crying for adventure, which can only be found by embarking on your own personal journey of self-discovery. You will discover your sense of adventure in a state of solitude, not in a relationship. Your sense of adventure will carry over into the relationship, but can never, genuinely be found there to begin with. You create your own sense of adventure. Your heart may never be free enough to really *be* adventurous until, at your new level of awareness, you recognize the value of love-of-self. Within this very personal accomplishment you will discover the richest source of self-esteem and unconditional love. Then comes the adventure!

~ Larry James

By Yourself. . . Alone Again?

❤

**LARRY
JAMES**

If you have recently come out of a relationship, heed this word of caution. It may be wise to distance yourself from relationships for a while. Take a breather. The tendency is often to quickly find someone else to be with. Most mental health professionals agree that this is not a good idea.

Cease and desist participation in the Desperation Derby. It's a dangerous race to be in. Desperate people can do desperate things. For some, they become so afraid of being alone, that in desperation, they find themselves in a race to be in another relationship before enough time has passed for the wounds to heal from the last one. The end result of a premature love relationship is dependence.

For some people being in a relationship becomes their "drug of choice." They skip around from relationship to relationship. Some get stuck. They feel as though they always have to be in a relationship. They develop the dependency of "needing" a relationship. This is not healthy. Some people allow their feelings of insecurity about being alone to keep them stuck, often in an unhealthy relationship.

Take some time out to see who you've become as a result of being in the relationship. Do you call it good or do you call it bad? Was there growth in some areas? What did you learn from being in the relationship? Will your next one be different? In what way?

Our former relationships never cease to provide us with new and exciting questions, the answers to which can lead to the breakthrough necessary for a healthy love relationship in the future. The rewards of personal inquiry are in-

LoveNote. . .

The essence of intimacy is feeling closer to yourself while you are in a healthy love relationship with someone other than yourself.

~ Larry James

LoveNote. . .

Only those who can live alone are able to live well with another.

~ Taz W. Kinney

LoveNote. . .

Love is letting go of fear.

~ Gerald Jampolsky, M.D.

valuable and can assist us greatly in being ready for another relationship when the time is right.

I believe that every relationship we are in serves a definite purpose. It fulfills a need for us as we fulfill needs for someone else. Remember, we should only look back to see how far we've come or to see how much we've learned. Hopefully, we can look at our past love relationships and focus on the good we learned from them. I must admit, that at times this may be difficult.

Spend time working on you. Work on developing your own self as an individual. Reinvent a relationship with yourself. Make it a new and exciting relationship; one you can be proud to carry over into your next relationship with someone else. Nobody wants damaged goods.

Allow time for the healing that is necessary for you to feel comfortable with being alone. That is the only way you can learn how to really *be* with someone else in the future. I don't know about you, but after being in a love relationship, it is normal to feel rather insecure for a while. You may not want to admit it, but it's true.

It takes a while to adjust to your new beginning. The delayed gratification is worth it. One of the rewards is discovering that the more time you take for yourself, the more love you will have to give to your future love partner.

Choose to be alone for awhile. Being independent enough to be alone is a virtue. Cultivate it. When you can learn to be comfortable with being with yourself, then you may be getting closer to being ready for a healthy love relationship with someone else. During this time of aloneness you will discover a clear distinction of being lonely and being alone.

It is not unusual to experience feelings of loneliness while you are alone. However, the more time you spend getting in touch with who you are, the easier it will be for you to understand that you do not have to feel lonely when you

LoveNote...

I am insecure to the degree I keep parts of myself hidden from myself.

~ Hugh Prather

LoveNote...

Our feelings help us to discover ourselves. Heed their call. They provide clues and insights into who we are and often become the catalyst for re-inventing ourselves. The energy for change is inspired by the emotional honesty we express through our feelings.

~ Larry James

LoveNote...

Fear is neither an intelligence I wish to lead me nor a sin I wish to flee. It is a great churning of thought caused by the object of thought, and only stillness can see past it. However, it is not the fearful thoughts themselves that must be stilled, but thoughts containing stillness that must be brought into focus.

~ Hugh Prather

are alone. Some people can feel lonely in a crowd. Feeling lonely is a choice. You can choose to feel one way or another. It is totally up to you. It depends on how you feel about yourself.

Being alone can help you in getting comfortable about being with yourself. When you are comfortable about being with yourself, your feelings of loneliness will gradually disappear. Instead of quickly looking for someone else, it may be a much wiser choice to choose to be okay with being alone for a while. Spend some time learning to be good company with yourself.

Pretend we can freeze a frame in our relationship movie. We are in the leading role. We can't believe what we are seeing. This time we are not acting. We really are afraid. We experience mixed emotions. We see ourselves, frozen with the fear of being alone and at the same time we want to be with a love partner yet we are afraid to really let ourselves *be* with someone else. I mean, really *be* with them.

Avoid the self-created fear of being alone. Accept that we do this to ourselves. It can bring no good into our lives. We allow fear to cause us to withhold ourselves from others. Fear breeds insecurities.

It could be said, for example purposes, that even Tarzan, Lord of the Jungle was insecure. He would swing from vine to vine, not letting go until the next vine was safely in hand. Does this sound familiar? This may make sense when you are in the jungle. When you are swinging high above the ground, your life depends on it.

Your life does not depend on always being in a relationship. The need to always be swinging from one love partner to another is not in your best interest. If you are coming *from* a love relationship, the last thing you need is another one... right away, that is. In this scenario, there is no safety in numbers.

We are so afraid of finding ourselves hanging in mid-air,

How
To
Really
Love
the
One
You're
With!

LoveNote. . .

Every individual needs a period of aloneness or solitude
in order to cope with the increasing pressures of life. . .
Do not encroach upon one another's independence.
~ Paramahansa Yogananda

LoveNote. . .

The more I attempted to "be me" the more "me's" I found
there were. Now I understand that to be myself means
consciously choosing which level of my feelings I am going to respond to and recognizing that, whatever I am
feeling, I am always free to think carefully rather than
carelessly about myself and those around me.
~ Hugh Prather

LoveNote. . .

Let him who cannot be alone beware of community. . .
Let him who is not in community beware of being alone.
~ Dietrich Bonhoeffer

we latch onto the first available vine that happens along. Not a good idea!

Leap into your greatest fear. . . be by yourself for a while. Take a good look at what "hanging in mid-air" feels like. You may be surprised! You will be okay. It won't be the end of the world. Although it may feel like it, that feeling won't last forever.

It is wise to practice intimacy with "self" during your abstinence from relationships. Get to know you. Give yourself the gift of solitude. Fall in love with yourself for a change and see how great that feels! Be your own significant other. Practice the art of loving you. Take the precious time out that is necessary to rediscover who you are *without* a love partner.

You must first learn to be alone and happy before you can be together and happy. Learn that it is possible for you to live alone and not be lonely. Discover how to be self-sufficient. Don't be dependent on others for your own existence.

Know that when you eventually do connect with someone you can love, your happiness will be enhanced just knowing that being in the relationship is your choice and not something you must have to survive. To have found someone you can share your life with is one of love's ultimate adventures.

Not having a relationship doesn't keep you all warm and cuddly at night, however, getting yourself ready for a really great love relationship must be your highest priority. Being true to yourself first is well worth the effort.

Get comfortable with being with you. If you are uncomfortable being with yourself, what makes you think anyone else would ever want to be with you?

Being alone can call up all of the feelings you were afraid

How
To
Really
Love
the
One
You're
With!

LoveNote. . .

Most of us in committed, stable relationships settle for predictability, comfort, and companionship because we fear exploring the mysteries that we embody together as man and woman, the exposure of our deepest selves. Yet in our fear of the unknown within us and between us we ignore and avoid the very gift that our commitment sets within our reach - true intimacy.

~ Robin Norwood

LoveNote. . .

What the fool does in the end, the wise man does in the beginning.

~ Japanese Proverb

LoveNote. . .

Love is not primarily a relationship to a specific person; it is an attitude, an orientation of character which determines the relatedness of a person to the world as a whole, not towards one 'object' of love.

~ Erich Fromm

you would have if you were ever alone. . . and some you could have never imagined. The pain seems to go on and on and only if you allow it. Healing takes time. Stay with solitude. Don't be tempted.

At the end of your tunnel is love-of-self and healing. You must attain this awareness before you can be in a healthy love relationship with someone else. In times like these, when you are alone with your feelings, life can feel empty.

Attention is not the answer to emptiness. Calling attention to ourselves or having to always be with someone at a time when we need solitude is not the answer.

Why is it that when we most need the quiet that is necessary when we self-examine, we feel the need to fill our lives with noise and frantic activity? What are we afraid of? Face it. We must stand firm and face the truth about who we are. . . alone.

Quiet, please. Peace of mind and contentment can only be found in silence. It is the time when you dedicate the moment to yourself; the time when you make time to really get to know yourself through self-inquiry.

You can gain much insight into the power of your attitudes in the stillness of looking inward. Your body believes every word you say. Your words and thoughts govern how you feel today and how you will feel tomorrow. A quiet and peaceful mind takes form as a quiet and peaceful body.

Many of your most intimate experiences are not with other people but with yourself. They come in those moments when you discover something new about who you are or who you are being. Self is experienced only in intimacy with self.

See what it feels like to walk hand in hand with yourself. Give yourself permission to do what may feel risky. Discover new ways of thinking and being. To allow intimacy

How
To
Really
Love
the
One
You're
With!

LoveNote. . .

It takes courage to grow up and turn out to be who you really are.

~ E. E. Cummings

LoveNote. . .

Love yourself exactly as you are and you are forever changed. Love others exactly as they are and they are free to change.

~ Kathlyn and Gay Hendricks

to be present in a relationship with another, you must first seek intimacy with yourself.

Some of our most clear thinking about relationships can be when we are not in a relationship. Our mind is often sharper when informed by our own feelings. We are more humble and acutely more in touch with the hurts of the past. We are far more open to new ideas.

Take advantage of this opportunity to learn all you can about yourself and what makes a healthy love relationship. It is in the search for what it takes to have a healthy love relationship that we become more receptive to listen for new ways to make our relationships work better in the future. The very process of searching opens up many new options.

Make having a relationship with yourself your number one priority. Then, and only then, can you move on to what's next!

LoveNote. . .

Love is seldom spontaneous, instant, dynamic. It usually takes considerable time to create. It results from work, from thinking, from promoting equality, from being able to cope and adapt.

~ William Lederer

LoveNote. . .

Start from where you are. Don't look back. Begin again. This is it! Fresh beginnings must always be looked forward to with hope. The rewards are incalculable.

~ Larry James

Start From Where You Are

**LARRY
JAMES**

♥

Losing yourself in a love relationship is not always what it seems. By most standards, it is not healthy *and* it's not the end of the world. You will bounce back. It may take some time *and* you can do it. As a matter of fact, the search to find yourself again can yield a great more personal insight than you might imagine.

After we have experienced losing ourself in a love relationship, we tend to look for our old self again. . . to go back to who we were before we were in the relationship. This doesn't work.

There is nothing worth going back for. There is no old self to go back to. There is only you, now. This is it! Push forward. Remembering who you were only keeps you stuck. It has you concentrate on more of what didn't work. Why would you want to mentally rehearse what you don't want? What you focus on, you get more of.

You will always be further ahead if you start from where you are. Look for answers that can forward the action of a healthy love relationship. The secret can be found in the search. Look within, a place where you might never remember to look. Don't cheat yourself out of this worthwhile experience.

Upon closer examination you can begin to see that the original losing of self, in effect, is the only road back to where you were when you thought you lost yourself.

Focus on the rewards of beginning again. . . of starting where you are right now. Do so with gusto! Focus with concentrated effort on loving yourself. A relationship with self is a prerequisite to having a healthy love relationship with someone else.

**How
To
Really
Love
the
One
You're
With!**

LoveNote. . .

Love is but the discovery of ourselves in others, and the delight in the recognition.

~ Alexander Smith

Looking Out For #1

♥

Never allow anything to have a higher priority than looking out for number one. You are all you have. Never allow
anyone, not even your love partner, to rob you of the single
most important personal responsibility of your life. You
must take care of you first. Only then will you be ready to
face the daily realities of a love relationship.

Taking care of you first is a lifelong project. It is a lifetime
commitment. It must be your top priority; your most specific intention. Don't take this one lightly.

Me first is not selfishness. It is not narcissism. Common
sense says, "If I don't take care of me, who will?" Me first
is only what it says. It says, "I care enough about me to
make sure that my needs get met and that I will always only
depend on myself for myself."

If you are looking for someone who will do this for you,
forget it. *Healthy* love relationships aren't made up that way.

You never have to apologize or make excuses for taking
care of you. Be careful about talking about how tough things
are and how hard you work and how little time you have.
Never be ashamed to tell people that you took a little time
out for yourself. There is nothing wrong with looking out
for number one, first.

If you have been in an unhealthy relationship, take care not
to repeat the destructive behaviors of the past that brought
you to this point.

We can get so busy working on trying to fix our love partner - an impossible task, I might add - that we forget that
we are responsible for only fixing ourselves. Often we give

How
To
Really
Love
the
One
You're
With!

LoveNote. . .

In jealousy there is more self-love than love.
~ Chinese Fortune Cookie

ourselves so completely to our love partner we lose track of who we are and what we need for our own fulfillment in the relationship.

One of the reasons this happens is because we place more value on others than we place on our own well-being. We are more concerned about what others think of us than what we think of ourselves. Depending upon others for our feelings of self-worth is a major step in the wrong direction. I believe this scenario is initiated by our self-defeating thoughts and manifested by our self-defeating behavior.

Those who still can't get it keep doing the same old things and getting the same old results. They scratch their heads and wonder who they are and what in the world is going on. They haven't the foggiest notion that they may be the only problem.

Who would you have to become to take care of you first?

Think about it.

As you begin looking out for number one - really paying attention to you - your sense of self is elevated to a new plateau of awareness. You begin to rediscover those feelings of accomplishment you have hidden from yourself for so long; perhaps hidden by your lack of understanding about how important it is to accept the 'me first' philosophy.

You begin to feel better about you! That feels good so you begin to have fun being yourself once more. Your attitude about yourself is getting better. You feel good about who you are. You discover you are changing, people are noticing and it feels good. You regain your zest for living. Your attitude becomes, "Ain't life great! Let's go have some fun!"

High self-esteem is attractive to others.

There is only one exception I can think of. If the other person has low self-esteem, they may feel very uncomfortable in the presence of someone who knows what they want,

**How
To
Really
Love
the
One
You're
With!**

LoveNote. . .

Resolve to romance a life lived with balance.

~ Larry James

LoveNote. . .

Love is not a problem, not an answer to a question. Love knows no question. It is the ground of all, and questions arise only insofar as we are divided, absent, estranged, alienated from that ground.

~ Thomas Merton

where they are going and what kind of relationship they want. They may feel intimidated by you. I say, "So what?" They may not be the kind of person you want to be around anyway.

Again, forget trying to fix them. You can't do that anyway. Only you can fix you.

When I say pay attention to you or take care of yourself first, I am not talking about self-centeredness. Self-centeredness breeds indifference to others. The arrogance of *only* looking out for yourself will find you being passed over in the relationship department.

I am talking about making a contribution to yourself with the same fervor and generosity you would for your love partner. Preoccupation only with self can leave both you and your lover very lonely. It is wise to pay as much attention to the needs of your love partner as you do to your own.

Balance is a prerequisite and a goal worthy of pursuit.

**How
To
Really
Love
the
One
You're
With!**

LoveNote. . .

I don't know what is best for you. I trust you to know that. I know what is best for me. And I trust you to trust me.

~ Natasha Josefowitz, Ph.D.

LoveNote. . .

When a love relationship allows no room for personal growth, it cannot be a healthy one.

~ Larry James

LoveNote. . .

Being able to share yourself in an atmosphere of safety and trust is the key to overcoming the fear that inhibits love.

~ Harold H. Bloomfield, M.D.

Trust Yourself

♥

LARRY JAMES

We must learn to trust ourselves enough to *be* the person who can accomplish what we want in a healthy love relationship. Then, and only then, can we be free to *do* the things necessary for our reality to become what we desire it to be.

Trusting yourself is an essential part of contribution in a healthy love relationship. For your relationship to mature, you must trust yourself enough to share yourself fully with the one you love. Trust is what makes sharing yourself with another possible.

Trust stands behind a guarantee that the giver will never lose, only gain. To hold sacrifice higher than giving is to scoff at the very idea of trust.

Trusting yourself breeds courage. Self-disclosure demands some risk of getting hurt. Your demonstration of courage, that is. . . revealing your true self to your love partner, in an atmosphere of unconditional love and acceptance, can open up new conversations that will support further disclosure in the most sensitive areas of your relationship, perhaps in the areas that count the most.

Trust yourself unconditionally. To the degree that your trust is conditional, you will have unrealistic expectations. That is not trusting yourself. You will find yourself getting in the way of what you say you want. Trust yourself. Stay out of your own way. And trust a higher power, with no strings attached. Trust God and *do* something!

Learning to trust yourself is to accept yourself for who you are. Trusting yourself enough to withhold nothing; to be

**How
To
Really
Love
the
One
You're
With!**

LoveNote. . .

To love yourself as you are, you must let go of, disengage
from, all thoughts and feelings about how you really
should be.

~ Paul Williams

LoveNote. . .

No value-judgement is more important to humans - no
factor more decisive in their psychological development
and motivation - than the estimate one passes on oneself.

~ Nathaniel Branden

totally open with your lover is both mutually and emotionally enriching. Not everyone, however, is ready for the kind of openness trust creates. Trust works best when it is mutually enjoyed.

To your love partner, not withholding could be perceived as "moving too fast." This could mean the beginning of the end. People are different. Situations are never the same. Trust yourself to say what needs to be said, when it needs to be said. Slow down a bit. Test the water and remember not to use testing the water as a cop out. Live life full out. Life is too short to withhold yourself from those that you care about.

In spite of all your efforts to ease into not withholding, some people will pull away. When you feel this happening, take time to have a conversation about it. Let people know what's on your mind. More than likely, they have similar feelings, yet are afraid to confront them. So, they distance themselves from you, which, in effect, constructs a barrier only love and loving conversation can break through.

When you have tried loving conversation and your love partner is still affected by your openness, you have a choice to make. If you allow being with your love partner to inhibit you in being who you are, it may be time to reach some new agreements or choose someone new to be with. It may be necessary to move on to what's next.

**How
To
Really
Love
the
One
You're
With!**

LoveNote...

It is by believing in roses that one brings them to bloom.

~ French Proverb

LoveNote...

Love is seldom spontaneous, instant, dynamic. It usually takes considerable time to create. It results from work, from thinking, from promoting equality, from being able to cope and adapt.

~ William Lederer

Design A Relationship With Yourself

♥

LARRY JAMES

Never allow the person closest to your heart to keep you from your own personal breakthrough in the relationship you have with yourself. Stay true to yourself. Stay tuned in to who you are. Keep your own counsel.

Stay focused on *your* design of the relationship. Re-examine this design consistently. Is it working? Invent new ways to improve it.

Random mental images without design result in reality randomly expressed. Something is wrong with that picture. Be clear about what you want in your love relationship and be clear that random doesn't work!

You have the power. Use it. Use it to your best advantage. Use it for the benefit of all concerned. Quietly anticipate the desired outcome.

The relationship of your heart's desire will manifest itself when you, in earnest, expect it to happen and then consistently do everything you can to make it happen.

LoveNote. . .

If we believe we shall fail, it is because we have sold ourselves on that belief. By the same process, we can sell ourselves on the belief that we shall succeed in whatever goal we set out to accomplish. When we succeed, what are the *benefits*? Believe in *them*. Life is a mirror reflecting to us, as conditions, the images of our inner expressions of thought.

~ Larry James

LoveNote. . .

A (love relationship) plan eliminates discontent by promising change. Ironically, a plan is only a decision to imagine a different future, and if followed too rigidly it blocks your sensitivity to the people around you.

~ Hugh Prather

Make Some Plans. . . Together!

♥

LARRY JAMES

One reason people are unsuccessful in setting relationship goals is that sometimes they don't know what they want until they know what they don't want. Not setting goals is a workable method of getting more of what you don't want. It works every time.

If you don't set relationship goals, you will always be wondering what tomorrow holds. When you get sick and tired of that, you will do something different. Most likely, not before.

My own personal experience has been that when I set relationship goals; when I decide what I want in a healthy love relationship, I begin to get excited about what tomorrow will bring. I begin to experience a knowing that comes from having made a decision to do something different; a knowing that tells me that I am the one who is in charge here. I live my choices. I call the shots. If it is to be, it is up to me. What an awesome discovery! *I can make a difference!* And I have to make that difference for me before I can make a difference with anyone else.

Be flexible. Cast not your love relationship goals in bronze. Things change. So do people. Attitudes change. *And* we are in charge of our own individual attitudes. Be sensitive to your love partner. Learn to adjust. It is important to have similar relationship goals. This makes it a little easier to relate to the differences that are always present in any love relationship.

Not setting goals causes anxiety about your relationship. A well laid plan eliminates discontent by promising the possibilities of a brighter future. It is a decision to reinvent

LoveNote. . .

Success is best achieved when you are clear about your goal but flexible about how to get there.

~ Brian Tracy

LoveNote. . .

Interests change. Friendship based on mutual interests is doomed. Real friendship is an unshakeable faith in what was once truly seen, no matter how recently or long ago.

~ Hugh Prather

your life together; to mutually imagine, then live the kind of relationship others only dream about.

So now you know. If you decide to press on and do something with this new-found knowledge, start by making a list of what you want in your relationship. When you complete this book you may want to go back and re-read Part I. Highlight the parts that you can accept as your own and get in bed with them. Study them until they become a part of you. When you work together on your relationship plan, you will find yourself getting down to the business of doing what must be done to accomplish what you both want.

Life is too short. You must harvest hay while the sun shines. You both will soon be too busy having fun; doing what you love and doing what matters to each other to ever have a concern about whether things will work out. Making plans and working together helps eliminate anxiety about your future together.

Here is the way to give your relationship a big bonus. Make sure some of your own personal goals are designed to contribute to your love partner *and* to your relationship. When you do good stuff for your love partner, you do good stuff for yourself!

LoveNote. . .

A love relationship anchored in unconditional love can survive the roughest storm. Trust puts you in the same boat. . . side-by-side. . . working on learning to trust, and trusting. . . *together!* Trust has you both rowing in the same direction.

~ Larry James

Trust

♥

LARRY JAMES

You can never be sure of the kind of relationship that is possible with another until you allow yourself to speak trust in the relationship. The possibility of trust lives in the speaking of it.

Knowing this does not make a difference. Doing it does.

Trust is fundamental to all human relationships. It is essential for effective communications, and is the foundation for continuity in a love relationship. Trust teaches us to relate to the one we love. It is necessary for a relationship to survive.

To trust is often scary. It assumes you must allow others the freedom to draw their own conclusions, make their own assessments, and interpret in their own way the openness that trust creates. Being okay with this is the acid test of trust.

Trust demands vulnerability and yet seems to simultaneously short-circuit it. It feels risky, like hanging in mid-air. Trust often feels like you are living on the edge. The more trust that is present in the relationship, the less vulnerable you feel.

For love relationships to sustain their sense of vitality, aliveness and zest they must be grounded in the trust that unconditional love nurtures. Trust insists on honest, open communication.

Trust demands no withholds. It invites personal disclosure. When you trust the one you're with, you can step in front of the person you've been, allow your lover to see the real you and be more of your true self. You can more lovingly

How
To
Really
Love
the
One
You're
With!

LoveNote. . .

Patience is natural to those who trust.

~ A Course in Miracles

express how you think and feel when trust is present and feel more free to do so.

We all live in a box. Everything we know and have learned to trust in is in there with us. Trust requests that we open the door of the box we live in to discover new areas in which to develop trust. We must learn to trust ourselves enough to walk outside and slam the door. . . and stay there!

Trust gently nudges you toward the arena of fearlessness.

Forget testing the water. Just do it!

Trust.

There is a door to your heart that opens with trust and closes when you are afraid. Love can eliminate the fear of trusting, for fear cannot exist in the presence of love.

Trust blazes new trails. It opens up new opportunities to really *be* with the one you love.

Mistrust brings out the worst in us. Being trusted tends to bring out the best in us. We will usually do everything within our power to live up to the healthy expectations of our love partner.

Trust commands that you live in the present, trusting one moment at a time. To fully trust takes time and mature, committed love.

Trust elevates you to a new level of maturity. It calls attention to our willingness to listen to our inner wisdom, that still, small voice within; the one that never leads you astray. Do the work necessary to learn to trust yourself enough to listen to this voice.

Trust introduces you to a new freedom - the freedom to think and feel and really *be* with the one you love. Trust opens the door to unlimited possibilities.

Trust creates breakthroughs in having relationships work.

**How
To
Really
Love
the
One
You're
With!**

LoveNote...

Trust brings lovers together. Consider it a Divine joining; the inevitable interweaving that occurs when two
people love unconditionally and become as one. A feeling of deep inner security comes from the trust that is
present with unconditional love; a love that is
unnegotiated.

~ Larry James

Among lovers, trust invites the spark of the Divine to ignite their passion!

Trust keeps the magic of love alive.

Allowing trust to presence itself is the only true path to a healthy love relationship. An open, honest and loving relationship always begins with acceptance and understanding and evolves to trust!

Belief deserves a mention here. Often before you can trust again, you must first learn to believe in yourself once more. What may be needed is a deeper relationship with yourself... a plunge inward. Belief in yourself pushes you toward trust.

When you find yourself unwilling to trust yourself with open communication with another, consider first looking for someone who can believe and trust in you; one who will support you in that lesson until you can learn to trust yourself again. Trust carries you beyond belief. It is a journey into knowing.

You cannot give away what you do not have. When you love yourself, you can give love away. When you come to a place where you can trust yourself, you can then trust enough to share yourself fully with the one you love.

Trust is often a difficult lesson to learn *and* it is one of the most rewarding. It opens up a whole new set of possibilities for you to consider. *And you get to make the choices.* How exciting!

Trust brings lovers together. Consider it a Divine joining; the inevitable interweaving that occurs when two people love unconditionally and become as one. A feeling of deep inner security comes from the trust that is present with unconditional love; a love that is unnegotiated.

There can be no unconditional love without trust. Arms-length trust does not work. Withholding trust creates a barrier around your heart.

LoveNote...

One word frees us from the weight and pain of life; that word is love.

~ Sophocles

LoveNote...

When we are getting along well we say we are connecting. When we are connected we love being together, we talk easily and laugh freely, we touch each other naturally and lovingly, we encourage each other, we celebrate each other's uniqueness, we serve each other joyfully and we tease each other playfully.

~ Bill & Lynne Hybels

A relationship without trust is guarded. . . it is tainted by a lack of full self-expression with the one you love.

A love relationship anchored in unconditional love can survive the roughest storm. Trust puts you in the same boat... side-by-side. . . working on learning to trust, and trusting... *together!* Trust has you both rowing in the same direction.

If you want an adventurous heart experience in which the thirst for love is quenched forever by a love relationship blessed with unconditional love. . . *trust is the only answer.*

Trust is the most powerful conversation for intimacy in a relationship. Trust creates the opening for intimacy to exist.

Where trust is present in a love relationship you will find two hearts dancing. . . another true miracle of love.

**How
To
Really
Love
the
One
You're
With!**

LoveNote. . .

Maturity is wanting nothing but what we see with the purity of our heart.

~ Hugh Prather

LoveNote. . .

To be capable of real love means becoming mature, with realistic expectations of the other person. It means accepting responsibility for our own happiness or unhappiness, and neither expecting the other person to make us happy nor blaming that person for our bad moods and frustrations.

~ John A. Sanford

LoveNote. . .

Aging is inevitable. Maturing is optional.

~ Hallmark Contemporary Card

Maturity in Relationships

♥

LARRY JAMES

Maturity, in general, is many things. Maturity in a love relationship is everything! First it is the ability to base a decision about a love relationship on the big picture - the long haul. In general, it means being able to pass up the fun for the moment and select the course of action which will pay off later.

In a love relationship, it means being able to enjoy the instant gratification that comes with the romance of the moment while knowing the best is yet to be and being patient while you watch your love grow. It is knowing that by working together, the state of unconditional love will presence itself in the relationship and will mature with time. It is knowing that you grow into a love relationship. It doesn't happen all at once. Mature love partners seek new ways to help each other grow.

One of the characteristics of infancy is the "I want it now" approach. Grown-up people can wait. And often they don't. Often they allow themselves to slip back into infancy so they can justify rushing into things.

Maturity is the ability to stick with a project or a situation until it is finished. It means doing whatever it takes to make the relationship be one you are proud to be in. The adult who is constantly changing jobs, relationships, and friends, is in a word. . . *immature*. They cannot stick it out because they have not grown up. Everything seems to turn sour after a while.

Mature love partners have learned not to expect perfection in each other. They know that acceptance has its own reward. Each lover's differences test the other's capacity for

149

LoveNote. . .

For a love relationship to mature, both partners must experience a deep feeling, a tacit belief, that there is something quite special about them which would never have happened had each not contributed to its creation.

~ Larry A. Bugen

LoveNote. . .

It is a sorry day when we give up what is best in ourselves, when we sacrifice the values and ideals that give our lives meaning, for some temporary advantage.

~ Michael Lynberg

LoveNote. . .

Young love is a flame - very pretty - often very hot and fierce, but still only light and flickering. The love of the older and disciplined heart is as coals, deep-burning, unquenchable.

~ Henry Ward Beecher

acceptance, forgiveness and understanding. They never dance around issues. When necessary, they discuss their imperfections, lovingly, with care not to pass judgement with harmful words. Acceptance and tolerance hold hands in the presence of unconditional love.

Mature lovers - lovers who love unconditionally, develop a knack for side-stepping resentment and focus on the good they see in one another. They have evolved to a higher level of understanding, one that transcends taking notice of the imperfections of the other.

Maturity is the capacity to face unpleasantness, frustration, discomfort and defeat without complaint or collapse. The mature love partner knows they can't have everything their own way. They are able to defer to circumstances, to other people - and to time, when necessary.

Mature love partners permit each other the freedom to pursue their individual interests and friends without restriction. This is when trust presents itself. Mature love allows this level of separateness to bring lovers closer together. In this scenario separateness is perceived as a bond, not a wedge. It encourages love partners to celebrate their own uniqueness.

Maturity is the ability to live up to the responsibilities of a love relationship, and this means being dependable. It means keeping your word; it means living in your relationship like your word really means something. Dependability equates with personal integrity. This means no withholds. It means saying what needs to be said, with love. Do *you* mean what you say? Do *you* say what you mean?

The world is filled with people who can't be counted on; people who never seem to come through in the clutches; people who break promises and substitute alibis for performance. They make excuses. They show up late - or not at all. They are confused and disorganized. Their lives are a chaotic maze of unfinished business and uncommitted relationships. Oh, what a tangled web we weave.

**How
To
Really
Love
the
One
You're
With!**

LoveNote. . .

Love waits on welcome, not on time.

~ A Course in Miracles

LoveNote. . .

Mature love offers us our most profound opportunity for regaining wholeness - not because our partners will fill all of our emptiness, but because we can use the embrace of a loving relationship to nurture ourselves toward greater maturation and ripening.

~ Larry A. Bugen

LoveNote. . .

We can come to realize that mature love equals loving yourself for being what you are, and likewise loving another person for who they are. When we can feel such unconditional no-matter-how-you-act love, we have learned what I call mature love. Mature love allows you fully to be yourself with your loved one.

~ Bruce Fisher, Ed.D.

Maturity is the ability to make a decision and stand by it. Immature people spend their lives exploring endless possibilities and then do nothing. Action requires courage. There is no maturity without courage.

Maturity is the ability to harness your abilities and your energies and to do more than is expected in your relationships. The mature person refuses to settle for mediocrity. They would rather aim high and miss the mark than aim low and hit it.

LARRY JAMES

**How
To
Really
Love
the
One
You're
With!**

LoveNote. . .

If you could only love enough you would be the happiest
and most powerful being in the world.

~ Emmet Fox

No Withholds!

♥

It may be true that we often seek in others that which we are not willing to give ourselves. This is a correctable mistake. It is not a good reason to be in a relationship. If we are only being with someone for what they can do for us, that is called dependency.

What we think we lack, we think we will find in someone else. The sense of self we assume we lack can never happen by osmosis. What we think we need from others can never rub off on us. Being with a love partner who has the qualities we lack does not necessarily enable us to acquire those desired qualities ourselves.

It is simply only *your* choice to give yourself what you think you lack. What a wonderful gift. You deserve it! You do this through the awareness self-discovery inspires.

Being with someone who is independent will not cure our own leaning toward dependency. You must do this on your own. And preferably before entering into a new relationship. You alone hold the key to the cure.

It is time for us to know that we lack nothing. Nothing, except perhaps the insight to know that we already have everything there is, including that which we seek from someone else. We have only yet to discover it within ourselves. This takes time and patience and understanding and lots of love for ourselves. *And* you have to want to!

You must never withhold discovery of self from yourself.

It is important to give yourself the gift you have been withholding from yourself before you attempt a serious love re-

LARRY
JAMES

LoveNote. . .

Withholding what is in your heart slowly but surely shreds the fabric of trust. Sharing words of truth from the heart is the medium by which two lovers connect. It is the catalyst for a committed, healthy love relationship.

~ Larry James

lationship. You may discover that once deeply involved with a love partner, with all of the many nuances of a relationship, you may never again find time to concentrate on giving yourself what you think you need if you are in the throes of always putting your best foot forward in the relationship.

When we first meet, we want to look our best; we instinctively do our best to sell ourselves. We put aside our bad habits and turn into someone who is focused solely on looking good. Many of us never intentionally shift to this mode to deceive, but do so in an effort to impress our new partner.

Others become a chameleon. They become who they think their new love partner wants them to be; changing frequently, always attempting to live up to someone else's expectations.

This is a losing game. No one can win it. How frustrating this must be, not only for you but for your love partner as well. How confusing it must be to be with someone when you never know how they are going to be the next time you are with them. This kind of unpredictability will get you nowhere. The relationship is doomed from the beginning. You are lying to yourself. It is certainly not putting your best foot forward. It is a major withhold which is dishonesty in action.

This is not being who you really are. It is not being honest with the one you're with, and most certainly not being honest with yourself. It is withholding that side of you that must always eventually be revealed if two people are to really know each other. How can someone get to know you if you never reveal your true self to them?

Another tendency is to only see the good in our new love partner in the beginning. I believe it is totally appropriate to look for the good in everyone, however, by contrast, it is

**How
To
Really
Love
the
One
You're
With!**

LoveNote...

Love does not dominate; it cultivates.

~ Johann Wolfgang von Goethe

LoveNote...

And the day came when the risk to remain tight in a bud was more painful than the risk it took to blossom.

~ Anais Nin

a potentially unhealthy tendency to purposely overlook *what we do not want to see.*

We become carried away with the romance of it all. We hear bells and whistles and see shooting stars. We are moon-struck. Give it time and the negative seems to always surface. It is only a matter of time before the bubble bursts.

I choose to trust that my love partner can listen to the real me and know that what I reveal about myself is really who I am. I trust her to love me for who I am, not for who she thinks I should be.

Some may argue that there are certain things that you must never share with your love partner. Perhaps. That is a personal decision. However, if trust is to be present in your relationship, you must demonstrate your own personal integrity. For me, this means no withholds.

For purposes of this conversation, I am referring to letting your lover know who you really are. I do not mean revealing something you have done in your distant or not too distant past that is not relevant to your current situation. That is being irresponsible and may hurt your love partner or perhaps even destroy the trust that may be present now.

If you have things that you feel you *must* reveal to your love partner that may cast a permanent shadow over your relationship, you would be well advised to first seek the services of a professional therapist or spiritual leader before you make the final decision to do so.

If both love partners strive for a state of truly being who they are, without withholds, they will find that they can see both the negative and positive sides of each other early in the relationship. There is great value in this.

I believe it is possible to put your best foot forward and at the same time, very quickly allow your new love partner to see who you really are. It is risky.

LoveNote. . .

There is no fear in love; but perfect love drives out fear.

~ I John 4:18

LoveNote. . .

"I need your heart and your eyes and your ears and your touch and your words. I want you to see me and hear me and feel me and speak to me and love me." But by *giving* what I want, I realize that I have what I thought I lacked before.

~ Hugh Prather

We wonder, "If we let them see who we *really* are, will they go away?" The truth is, if we don't let them see who we really are they may go away anyway. All we see is a puff of smoke!

People love people who are real.

I would rather present myself for who I am. My love partner will either love me for who I am or she won't. I would rather make myself vulnerable, take the risk and know where I stand, than to withhold who I really am, only to have my love partner leave in six months because the me I withheld was not someone she was able to *be* with.

Make a mutual commitment to no withholds, another of the keys to success in a healthy love relationship.

How
To
Really
Love
the
One
You're
With!

LoveNote. . .

Love grows and matures when gentle words of love are spoken truthfully from the heart.

~ Larry James

LoveNote. . .

A commitment is more than an agreement. You make an agreement from your mind. You discover your commitment in your heart.

~ Bob Mandel

LoveNote. . .

Let us not love only in words or in talk, but let us put our love in action and make it real.

~ John 3:18

Commitment + Action

♥

LARRY JAMES

For you to achieve what you desire in a love relationship, both love partners must have similar levels of commitment. Each must honor a promise of mutual commitment to the other; a commitment to participate in life fully… together.

This does not mean that you must have identical commitments. It means that for a healthy love relationship to thrive and survive, each love partner must support the other in their own individual commitments in addition to their commitment to each other as a team. She is committed to something and he supports her. He is committed to something and she supports him.

When true love is present, commitments arise naturally. They expand our capacity to love.

The commitment that supports a healthy partnership is the commitment each has to the other to always be working on the relationship; a commitment to always be in a dance with one another, showering each other with compassion and understanding.

Commitment is nurtured by compassion and understanding.

If you care to move past commitment. . . try surrender. Surrender is one step *beyond* commitment.

Surrender does not mean placing yourself at the mercy of someone else. To me, surrender is the ultimate commitment to unconditional love; it is surrendering to the process, not to your love partner. Having surrender present in your love relationship means having a devotion to keeping the fire of your love burning. . . for each other.

LoveNote. . .

Romantic love is not an aberration, it is the heady stuff that launches ships and makes the world go round. It is a powerful taste of the Divine as we experience it in one another. It is also the necessary vision that allows one to be crazy and daring enough to make a commitment.

~ Gertrude Mueller Nelson

LoveNote. . .

There is no victory without the willingness to risk setbacks or total defeat; no conquest of unconditional love in a relationship without the sacred bond that comes from a total commitment to team.

~ Larry James

It is possible to give yourself fully *to* the relationship without losing your sense of self *in* the relationship. It empowers each of you when both love partners are willing to surrender to the moment; to those tender moments when you are unconditionally loving the one you are with. It promotes freedom of full self-expression.

You both must trust one another enough to allow each other the freedom to speak words of truth straight from the heart. Open, honest communication is just one of the many keys to a healthy love relationship.

Add to commitment a decision for action. That's when the adventure begins. If you only always know what you are committed to and never totally support each other in your commitments, you may rediscover the same ordinary relationship you may have experienced in the past. How boring!

Why not go for extraordinary? Or, if you are truly adventurous, go for outrageous! That is anything but boring.

Commitment plus action provides the momentum that can produce extraordinary results! It's doing what *can* be done to make a difference for each other. . . and having a commitment to do it together. Even when it feels like you don't want to.

Especially when you don't feel like it.

**How
To
Really
Love
the
One
You're
With!**

LoveNote. . .

When love is strong, a man and woman can make their bed on a sword's blade. When love grows weak, a bed of 60 cubits is not large enough.

~ The Talmud

Resolving Conflict

♥

Conflict is inevitable. How we handle it is what makes the difference. When the structure of a love relationship breaks down, while fault may not necessarily be evenly distributed, both partners must ultimately accept equal responsibility. You are in this together.

It takes two for a healthy love relationship to work and it takes two to perpetuate an unhealthy love relationship. Seek not to place blame. What difference will that make? You both know the truth about what happened. Who cares whose fault it is?

"I do!" she screamed, "You just can't imagine what a jerk he is!"

He quickly and angrily countered with, "I wouldn't be such a jerk if you wouldn't nag at me all the time!"

Blah! Blah! Blah!

Who cares whose fault it is? If you love each other, focus on solving the problem! What happened, happened. That's all! It's not healthy to make things up about why something happened or who did what to whom. Again. . . who cares?

The goal of resolving conflict in a relationship is not victory or defeat. It is reaching a mutual understanding that benefits both love partners. Resolving conflict brings love partners closer together. It allows for negotiation and compromise.

Specific conversations, designed to "talk things out" will

**How
To
Really
Love
the
One
You're
With!**

LoveNote...

All married couples should learn the art of battle as they should learn the art of making love. Good battle is objective and honest - never vicious or cruel. Good battle is healthy and constructive, and brings to a marriage the principles of equal partnership.

~ Ann Landers

LoveNote...

Acceptance tills the soil that allows for individuality to grow.

~ Larry James

assist you on your path of self-discovery and is also a useful tool for resolving conflict. It brings about a higher awareness of your love partner's wants and needs.

Constructive conversations help to avoid repeating the patterns of behavior that incite the controversy that problems create in the first place. It takes two, working together to explore workable solutions that ease the tension that occurs when problems arise in a relationship.

A determination to resolve conflict by conversation offers a chance for healing and promotes the opportunity to become closer to the one you love.

Men and women are different, or have you noticed? Cherish the differences. Learn to accept and *be* with or accept the things you cannot change about each other.

**How
To
Really
Love
the
One
You're
With!**

LoveNote. . .

A good relationship occurs because two people devote time and energy to practicing simple principles and techniques to sustain monogamous love.

~ Alan Loy McGinnis

Are You Doing the Best You Can?

♥

LARRY JAMES

Have you ever just sat down in your easy chair, crashed for the evening and while listening to your favorite Eddie Daniels CD, wondered what is going on that has made some of your relationships not work very well?

I have. When I began to get honest with myself about the answers, I could feel the tears beginning to well up. I felt the fear of "alone again?" inside. My first reaction was to fight to hold back the tears. I suppose I should just have a good cry and be done with it.

I wept.

That seemed like the thing to do at the time. No easy way out though. Only a temporary release. I got the sense that there was more work to be done.

And the music didn't help. It seemed to bring out the melancholy in me. It brought the sadness to the surface. I found it interesting that the title of the CD was "Breakthrough." I could have used one of those about then. I knew that I had not been giving my best in my relationships. No wonder they weren't working! My sadness was leading me to change.

It may be important to stop every once in a while and really let yourself feel sorry for yourself so you can have a greater appreciation for how good it feels when things are going well.

Schedule a one-minute pity party. *And* only for a moment. Get down and dirty. Let yourself feel what you are really feeling. You will be okay. It is okay for both women *and* men to shed a few tears.

LoveNote. . .

For one human being to love another: that is perhaps the most difficult of all our tasks, the ultimate, the last test and proof, the work for which all other work is but preparation.

~ Rainer Maria Rilke

LoveNote. . .

Love can only be kept by being given away, and it can only be given perfectly when it is also received.

~ Thomas Merton

Then get busy and make some changes in the way you are being and doing.

I believe that the most important thing for me is my power of choice. . . my option to feel however I choose to feel, do whatever I choose to do and be whoever I choose to be. Life lives on the tip of my tongue. Things go well because I say so. Unfortunately, the opposite is also true.

There is one major question to consider when you ponder how your relationships aren't working. *You must ask yourself if you are doing the best you can.*

I am not talking about giving your relationship your best shot when you feel like it. Are you really doing the very best that you can? Are *you* doing whatever it takes? Are you taking the time to develop your relationship and to develop within it? If time were your last five dollar bill, do you suppose you would be more careful how you spent it? All the money in the world will not buy back one lost minute. Give your best to your efforts every moment. You are the only one with the answers to these questions. It's time for self-honesty.

Refuse to give in to those feelings of discouragement and despair when things are not going the way you planned them. You have no good reason to be discouraged or to be in despair if you are doing the best you can. If you are doing the best you can and things consistently go wrong, consider that you may be doing the wrong things the best you can. Then, comes self-examination.

A successful, healthy love relationship is built on a solid foundation of honesty and integrity. Integrity begins at home; it starts with you. It means, first of all, being honest with yourself, when, in the past, perhaps you haven't always been. It means being that way, in the moment, regardless of how it feels or whether you want to or not. Honor your commitments.

Always do the best you can.

LoveNote. . .

The love we give away is the only love we keep.

~ Elbert Hubbard

LoveNote. . .

The main fact of life for me is love or its absence. Whether life is worth living depends on whether there is love in life.

~ R. D. Laing

LoveNote. . .

Live only in the thought of love for all and you will draw love to you from all.

~ Ralph Waldo Trine

Know What Turns You On

♥

LARRY JAMES

Know what you need from your relationship. Then proceed with confidence. Mutually discuss your needs.

Relationships fail when two people who have been in love stop meeting each other's needs. This is another reason for paying attention to each other as the relationship progresses.

Needs change. Be sensitive to the changing needs of your love partner and your own. Talk about the changes and how they affect each other. Healthy people communicate.

Happy and healthy relationships are usually made between happy and healthy people; people who were happy and healthy before they became love partners. They are those who were content to first be happy alone so they can be happy with someone else.

It is only natural to have a list of qualities that you would prefer your new love partner to have or guidelines for how you would like the relationship to be. Caution. Be flexible. Know where you will compromise and where there is no room for compromise, then draw your line and stand on it.

You must know what must be present in your relationship for happiness to be stimulated within you. Know what brings you pleasure, then communicate those needs.

It is possible to fall in love with many people on the way to a forever love relationship. To allow yourself to choose a love partner who doesn't share a major portion of the qualities you hold dear; who may not be in agreement with, at least, most of your guidelines, or who is not willing to compromise some of the things on their list for the love of two, may not be in your best interest. You could be setting yourself up for failure before you get started. Articulate your needs. . . often.

**How
To
Really
Love
the
One
You're
With!**

LoveNote. . .

Love is not the cause of good relationships, it is the consequence of good relationships.

~ William Lederer

LoveNote. . .

Real love has nothing in common with any of its opposites - just as the sun is not dependent on the moon for its light or warmth.

~ Guy Finley

LoveNote. . .

It can be very lonely when you are in a love relationship and only build walls instead of bridges.

~ Larry James

LoveNote. . .

I love you, not for what you are, but for what I am when I am with you.

~ Roy Croft

Remember, there are two people involved here. It takes two to tangle; two to always be working on the relationship together. Knowing what you want is a major first step. It will help you recognize the kind of love relationship you want when it shows up or help you to re-energize your current relationship.

It also takes more than just knowing what you want. As I said in my last book, *The First Book of Life$kills*, "Knowing something does not make a difference. Doing something with that which you know does."

I am convinced that we can come closer to a relationship of unconditional love when we affirm what we want as if we already have it, and working toward that aim, refuse to sit around and accept what happens as if we had absolutely nothing to do with it. Being responsible in a love relationship is another worthy aim. I have tried that sitting around business. It didn't work for me.

As *you* are, so goes the relationship. You are the relationship.

You have everything to do with how relationships work out. What you think about and speak about, you bring about. Our thinking makes it so. When you expect to have a healthy love relationship and you do whatever is necessary to have it be great, you usually get what you expect. Relationships work out the way relationships work out. Sometimes things go great. Sometimes not so great.

I believe that a relationship consistently worked on by two people who really love each other always works out better than a relationship where love partners have doubts or low expectations. Why would anyone want to be in a relationship if they had doubts about it or low expectations of it? There are many answers to that question and perhaps a few self-serving reasons. None of them truly justify or accurately portray a *healthy* love relationship.

For a relationship to succeed, it is important to know what turns you on and what turns you off.

How
To
Really
Love
the
One
You're
With!

LoveNote. . .

Oh, be careful of the words you speak!

~ David Ring

Weigh Your Words

♥

LARRY JAMES

It is a wise love partner who is aware of the potential damage loose words can cause. Words spoken in anger inflict wounds that sometimes take a long time to heal. Think first, then speak.

It is one thing to speak what you feel and quite another to speak what you feel without regard to the consequences of the pain that might accompany your words when spoken hastily to your love partner.

The words we express allow us to predict the predicaments that will occur in our relationships. It is wise to be careful of the words we think. Thinking them becomes a dress rehearsal for what we can expect to happen. Speaking them activates the law of cause and effect.

On the other hand, the words of encouragement, of understanding, of love, or any words that echo good will always elevate us to their own level. That is most likely a higher place than where we began. As often as you can, speak only words of love.

Relationships don't die by themselves. We kill relationships with inappropriate words; words from the head, not from the heart.

Words once spoken create our present reality. They can never be recalled. We must remember to think before we speak. We must carefully weigh the cost of speaking our thoughts randomly and without evaluating the possible outcome. Be considerate of your love partner.

Often our thoughts revert back to the "safe zone" . . . the

LoveNote. . .

Words in haste do love partners waste.

~ Larry James

LoveNote. . .

Love is always patient and kind; it is never jealous; love is never boastful or conceited; it is never rude or selfish; it does not take offense, and is not resentful. Love takes no pleasure in other people's sins but delights in the truth; it is always ready to excuse, to trust, to hope, and to endure whatever comes. Love does not come to an end.

~ I Corinthians 13:4-8

familiar. . . the way of being that we were before, and *that* didn't work.

When we insist upon thinking and speaking past thoughts as words, we find that they will dominate our attention and only keep us stuck. Mentally rehearsing what doesn't work, doesn't work, if you want your life to be great. It only more deeply internalizes what you don't want. Focus on what you want in your relationship!

In essence, we begin to believe that which we think is our very own new idea. In reality, most likely, those thoughts are from our past, and if concentrated upon, reoccur as our present and eventually as our future. Give it up! Make up some new and exciting ways of being. We must give up what we don't want in favor of what we would like to happen.

In the Bible, Job said, "The thing I feared has come upon me." Those words were an acknowledgement of the power of his negative thinking, spoken as his word, which eventually became his very own reality.

The power of the words we speak is proven daily in what shows up in our lives. The tendency is to place blame on the circumstances around us rather than accept responsibility that we authored the thoughts we spoke and that in speaking them as words, in truth, created our present condition.

Our outer results will never be any different unless we make internal changes in the way we think and take caution of the words we speak!

LoveNote. . .

Being an artist at romance does not require so much a sentimental and emotional nature as it requires a thoughtful nature.

~ Alan Loy McGinnis

Thoughtfulness

♥

LARRY
JAMES

How important it is to be thoughtful of the one you love. Keeping love alive requires an attitude of thoughtfulness. It's called 'paying attention' to your love partner.

Thoughtfulness is an admittedly promising idea. It will bring a smile to the face of your loved one. It adds sparkle to your relationship.

Some of the biggest challenges in relationships come from being thoughtless. Thoughtlessness will sabotage your friendships and your relationships.

Often when we think of what must be done to keep the fire of love burning, we forget that *we* are the ones who must fan the flames. Fan the flames with thoughtfulness and love and lots of other good stuff.

Remember to do the little things that will demonstrate your commitment to love the one you're with.

Stop by the florist on the way home and buy your sweetheart a single rose just to say, "I care." Make plans to spend a quiet dinner by candlelight, just the two of you. Have it catered in. Surprise your lover with a special love note on her pillow. Shave *before* you go to bed. Notice that he shaved before he came to bed.

Plan a surprise picnic in the park with all the trimmings: music, wine, a blanket, the works! Don't forget the corkscrew. Sit together under a tree and watch the squirrels.

Notice his cologne. Notice her earrings. Offer an unexpected compliment. Wash the dishes, vacuum the carpet

**How
To
Really
Love
the
One
You're
With!**

LoveNote. . .

Random acts of thoughtfulness keep the graceful flame of love burning. They often dazzle your lover with their brilliance. They inspire a compassionate, warm, wonderful, and loving way of being together. Our capacity to love in this way ultimately defines who we are.

~ Larry James

and fold the laundry while she is away. Light a fire in the fireplace, dim the lights, break out the pillows, and just hold each other.

When your lover is talking. . . listen.

Visit Frederick's of Hollywood or Victoria's Secret and buy her some sexy undergarments. Take his car to the car wash while he's busy doing something else. Chill a bottle of her favorite wine for an unplanned evening of warm conversation and relaxation. Curl up together in your favorite chair for a cozy cuddle or two. Plan to dance by the light of the moon.

Thinking thoughtful thoughts and doing thoughtful things enhances the happiness of your love partner. Doing neat things for people you love can be a source of happiness enrichment in your own life, too.

Notice. I did not say it will make your love partner happy. Only they can do that. It enhances their happiness. As a result, it also enhances your relationship. It brings out the best in both of you. It keeps you focused on all of the little things that make up all of the big things. It helps keep a relationship happy, full of love, healthy and absolutely alive with passion. That makes it worth all the effort.

If having a relationship that creates its own opportunity to be great appeals to you, create your own "thoughtfulness" list. Take turns dreaming up the most romantic and fun things to do together that call attention to thoughtfulness.

When you plan to be thoughtful, you will find more new and exciting ways to tickle the fancy of your lover than you could imagine. Thoughtfulness does not always have to be something you think of on the spur of the moment. There is nothing wrong with planning to be thoughtful until you develop the thoughtfulness habit; until thoughtfulness becomes a part of who you are and ultimately a way of life.

**How
To
Really
Love
the
One
You're
With!**

LoveNote. . .

Two important things are to have a genuine interest in people and to be kind to them. Kindness, I've discovered, is everything in life.

~ Isaac Bashevis Singer

LoveNote. . .

Your capacity to love others is closely related to your capacity to love yourself.

~ Bruce Fisher, Ed.D.

Engage in a never-ending quest to find new ways to express thoughtfulness to one another and watch your relationship rise to a new level of emotional intensity and passion. Create special moments that will make your relationship one to which others can aspire.

Thoughtful acts of kindness are seldom forgotten. They measurably enhance the quality of your love relationships.

How
To
Really
Love
the
One
You're
With!

LoveNote...

Love means to commit oneself without guarantee, to give oneself completely in the hope that our love will produce love in the loved person. Love is an act of faith, and whoever is of little faith is of little love.

~ Erich Fromm

One of Our Best Days

LARRY JAMES

♥

I can always, if I want to, find something in today that wasn't there yesterday that makes today "one of my best days!" Sometimes I really have to look hard and long to find it. When I decide to really pay attention, I can always find something good.

What would you think if when you said, "How are you doing?" someone answered, "This is one of my best days!"?

I don't know about you but my curiosity would get the better of me. I would want to know just what it was that had it be one of their best days. It seems to me this could open up a very positive and constructive conversation.

I tested this idea recently when I saw one of the managers of a hotel in the hallway. She asked me how I was doing and I said, "This is one of my best days!"

It's easy to say that when things are going well. That day was truly one of my best days. Everything I touched turned to gold. I was on cloud nine.

She wanted to know what made it one of my best days, so I told her. I was glad she asked.

As my friend listened, I could see her becoming excited for me. Before we were through talking we were both charged up about the conversation. She was smiling and interacting with me in a way I had never experienced before. I was happy she was interested in hearing about my good news. You would have thought that it all happened to her.

I was moved to think that if couples in a love relationship would only look for the one thing each day that made their

189

**How
To
Really
Love
the
One
You're
With!**

LoveNote...

Love does not consist in gazing at each other, but in looking outward in the same direction.

~ Antoine De Saint-Exupery

LoveNote...

The words of Jesus, "Love one another as I have loved you," must be not only a light to us but a flame that consumes the self in us.

~ Mother Teresa

relationship special for that day, what a difference that might make!

What if, at the end of the day, you are talking with your love partner and you both could share that this day has been truly "one of our best days!"? The very idea promotes positive momentum.

I can think of a lot of good reasons for getting involved in this kind of conversation. I cannot come up with one good reason not to. Can you imagine how good it will feel to be able to share fully and concentrate mostly on the events of the day that had it be great for both of you?

If you are always looking for the good that makes life better, you will surely always find it. You will also be motivated to do more of what makes life great together.

Have a specific intention to initiate this kind of conversation with your lover. Exploring the things that make your relationship special can only assist you both in developing a stronger commitment to doing the things necessary to always have something good to talk about. It will draw you closer together.

When you look at your relationship carefully, you can always find plenty to work on. Never repress the things that happen that make the relationship not so great. Talk about them. Mutually decide what you can both do to make things better. Always working to make things better, noticing the efforts of your love partner and cherishing the results is what contributes to making up. . .

"This is one of our best days!"

Positive words build positive momentum in your love relationship.

**How
To
Really
Love
the
One
You're
With!**

LoveNote. . .

All you need is love. Love is all you need.

~ The Beatles

LoveNote. . .

With love in you, you have no need except to extend it.

~ A Course in Miracles

Maggie and Fleischman

❤

LARRY JAMES

If you have ever watched TV's popular "Northern Exposure" you may have come to the conclusion that Maggie and Fleischman should never, ever get married. They would kill each other. One moment there is so much passion they can hardly keep their hands off each other and in the next episode Maggie is throwing things at him and punching him in the nose.

Couples who live their lives in this way have a need to be right, among other things. They may be nice people who are stubborn, self-centered and who seem to find no room for compromise. They would rather argue and win than ever stop to consider the consequences of the win. Truly no one wins in an argument. No one ever wins when someone has to lose.

When they begin to realize that it is much healthier to be happy than to be right, then they can get on with loving and living a happy, healthy life together.

Maggie and Fleischman may be a good example of a couple who could, with effort, make some major changes and settle into a warm, loving and very healthy love relationship. Nothing is impossible. Especially on TV. Stay tuned.

A not so good relationship can become a great relationship when two people have a powerful commitment to each other and devote the time and energy necessary to have it be that way. When you allow unconditional love to be present, you must listen to its voice for it makes the rules.

Making the shift to a healthy love relationship takes two people who love each other and who have a commitment to

**How
To
Really
Love
the
One
You're
With!**

LoveNote. . .

In a full heart there is room for everything, and in an empty heart there is room for nothing.

~ Antonio Porchia

LoveNote. . .

When the heart is flooded with love there is no room in it for fear, for doubt, for hesitation. And it is this lack of fear that makes for the dance. When each partner loves so completely that he has forgotten to ask himself whether he is loved in return; when he only knows that he loves and is moving to music - then, and then only, are two people able to dance perfectly in time to the same rhythm.

~ Anne Morrow Lindbergh

support the personal and spiritual growth of the other. It means sharing instead of arguing. It means loving your love partner even when they make it difficult for *anyone* to love them.

It also means that just because there is a broken heart, the rules do not change. For the benefit of compromise, they may bend a bit, ever so slightly. If something is unacceptable or causes pain it must be communicated. . . in a loving way. Wrongs must be acknowledged and new commitments negotiated.

The individual with the broken heart validates that it is broken by choosing to have it continue to feel that way. When you validate something you support its continued existence. Not a healthy idea.

Healthy, committed love partners will say, "I'm sorry. I was wrong," instead of walking away.

Then there are people who should never get together. They are the people who allow pride, ego and all sorts of silly things to get in the way of having an intimate, healthy relationship. They are unwilling to do anything differently. In the long run they end up only hurting each other. They end up being lonely when they are alone and they wonder why. They can't understand why they keep going through relationships like a baby goes through diapers.

They are in a lot of pain and can't understand that it is they who write the script and they have cast themselves in the starring role. Pain is part of the script they have written. They are the ones who seem to be preoccupied with being right. They continue to play the same role with different leading men or women. They forget that people are human. Human beings make "mis-takes" just like in the movies.

I will never understand why people don't understand. It is predictably called stupid to do the some old things over and

LARRY
JAMES

**How
To
Really
Love
the
One
You're
With!**

LoveNote. . .

To be a true, unconditional friend, your love must be
anchored in God's love. Your life with God is the inspiration behind true Divine friendship with all.

~ Paramahansa Yogananda

over and expect different results. Insane is a more accurate word.

Being in a healthy love relationship takes working at it, together, all of the time. It takes lots of love and commitment.

Love is the answer. Genuine unconditional love is the kind of love you know is there even when it doesn't feel like it. The kind that has no preconceived notions or undelivered communications. The kind that always delivers on its promise. The kind that you can stand on and know it will never let you down.

It is the kind of Love that is the ultimate expression of who you really are and whose very expression demonstrates who you are choosing to become.

LoveNote. . .

Happiness and love are just a choice away.

~ Leo Buscaglia

LoveNote. . .

The heart that loves is always young.

~ Greek Proverb

It Is Your Choice

♥

LARRY JAMES

When you are hurting, it is difficult to remember that you will always feel much better after you've completed the experience of the pain of loss. After my separation, I first considered the pain of loss something bad that was happening *to* me.

The better feeling came when I discovered the hurt was not something that was happening *to* me, it was something that I chose to feel during the grieving process.

When the hurt becomes too intense, you have new choices to make. You can do something or not do anything. It is your choice.

This is a time for understanding, acceptance, forgiveness, and unconditional love. An appreciation of self, along with an attitude of high self-esteem would also help to make things better. The point is, you always call the shot on how you feel.

"But," you say, "you have no idea what she did to me!"

There's a clue in that statement about how you feel about yourself. "She did to me!" sounds like blame to me. We even say things like, "I have a right to be angry!" You are right, you do, yet there is no need to justify our own anger. If you want to be angry, no one but you can keep you from being angry. Name it and claim it! It is your choice.

No one can do anything to you. Have you ever considered that you may allow yourself to think and say things like this to avoid taking responsibility for your feelings? Quit kidding yourself. The truth is, she may have done something.

LoveNote...

Only love can bring us peace. And the experience of love is a choice we make, a mental decision to see love as the only real purpose and value in any situation.

~ Marianne Williamson

That's all! She did that. It is *you* who choose to feel one way or the other about it.

We think that expressing our displeasure or anger is going to make a difference in what has already happened. Wrong. This is called making a scene. I do not mean that we should never express our feelings about situations that are unacceptable to us. What I am saying is, we can express our feelings without all of the drama if we choose to do so. Do without the drama. Excessive anger can harm us. It causes stress and worse.

What you can *be* with in life, lets you *be*. It is your choice.

**How
To
Really
Love
the
One
You're
With!**

LoveNote...

Any question - except "why" - is an inward journey that begins with: what, who, how, where and when. These are the elements necessary for self-inquiry. The answers are within. You must want to find them, to find them. You must be hungry for self-discovery and thirsty for the insight the answers reveal.

~ Larry James

Why Ask, "Why?"

♥

LARRY JAMES

You have to really want a healthy love relationship before you can be motivated to do whatever it takes, all of the time, to have it be that way. You always have to be working on your relationships. You cannot coast uphill.

When love is present and you work together, you can move forward with a velocity few love partners experience.

Always expect your relationship to be great. Pause now and then to give it an inspection. It is wise to inspect what you expect. Never stop analyzing how your relationships are working, how they aren't working, and what you can do to make them work better.

Notice. I did not say "why" they are not working. Who cares why? Why doesn't count anymore. By the way, I do not mean that you shouldn't attempt to identify the cause. When you eliminate the cause, the effect changes. However, *only* trying to understand why will keep you stuck.

Perhaps asking yourself what you can do to heal the relationship or to contribute more to make it better might be a better solution and a much quicker path to recovery. Many people become so devastated by loss of attention, loss of a love partner and many other losses you can imagine, they are unable to cope with looking beyond why.

"Why" questions lead us into being defensive about our past, even when we are doing everything we can to focus on doing our best in the present; even when we are aware that changes must soon take place; even when we know that if things don't get better, we are leaving.

How
To
Really
Love
the
One
You're
With!

LoveNote...

Don't hold on to anger, hurt or pain. They steal your energy and keep you from love.

~ Leo Buscaglia

LoveNote...

Courage. It takes courage! To have a healthy love relationship you must take a leap of faith. The faith is in the leap; the leap into the unknown. In that moment you decide. With all the love you possess as your support, you make the decision for change in the presence of fear. And in doing so, fear goes away. The miracle of the adventure lies in living life in the leap! Two hearts - committed to be true to the other - will carry one another safely to the other side.

~ Larry James

"Why" is a hook! "Why" asks us to justify something that hasn't been working. And we fall for it! We seem compelled to take a stand to defend a position doomed to failure. Many times that's what got us in our unpleasant circumstance to begin with. Discontinue wasting mental energy on trying to figure out why.

"Why" questions often allow blame to creep in while we temporarily postpone accepting responsibility for our own dilemmas. "Why" questions encourage us to hold on to all the reasons why something isn't working, rather than move forward to look for solutions. Not a good idea.

When we ask "why," we are usually stuck with the problem for a longer period of time because sometimes "why" is difficult to figure out. Why questions take longer to answer and the answers - when finally discovered - are more difficult to understand because part of asking why is to find out who is to blame.

Sometimes it is difficult to find agreement in the arena of blame. It could take some time. The activity of blame only avoids taking responsibility in the relationship for a while. Some people are blind to this fact.

Can you see how "why" questions can keep you stuck?

Any question - except "why" - is an inward journey that begins with: what, who, how, where and when. These are the elements necessary for self-inquiry. The answers are within. You must want to find them, to find them. You must be hungry for self-discovery and thirsty for the insight the answers reveal.

You will both move ahead much faster when you ask, "What can I do to make my love relationship better?", "Who would I have to become to have my love relationship be great?", "How can I best contribute to the relationship and to my lover?", "Where shall I begin?" and "When do we get started?"

How
To
REally
Love
the
One
You're
With!

LoveNote...

The supreme happiness of life is the conviction that we are loved; loved for ourselves, or rather, loved in spite of ourselves.

~ Victor Hugo

There can be times when you can never truly understand why something really happened. What happened, happened. It is a part of history that can only affect you in the present if you let it.

And this is now.

Why ask, "Why?"

"Why" may not be so important anymore.

What are you going to *do* about it?

How
To
Really
Love
the
One
You're
With!

LoveNote. . .

"Downhill is hard, too!"

~ Bruce McNichols

Downhill Is Hard, Too!

LARRY JAMES

❤

The Smith Street Society Jazz Band, the band of a musician friend from New York, is often asked to march in parades. After marching with the wind and the rain in their hair, in the snow and in the heat of summer, he and the band were weary of parades. The last parade they marched in was uphill most of the way. They were exhausted.

The band was called and once again asked to participate. When my friend complained about the parade route being mostly up hill the last time, the caller quickly added, "Don't worry. This time most of the parade is downhill!"

My friend said, "What? Are you crazy? Downhill is hard, too! As a matter of fact it's worse!"

Brilliant insight!

We want our relationships to run smoothly. We want things to level off. Forget the ups and downs. Give us somewhere in the middle. The least effort we have to expend, the better. Someday we won't have all of these problems and things will be easy. Give me a break! With this kind of attitude people will soon be saying, "Ha! Ha! You lose!"

His response made me think.

Climbing the mountain of life *is* difficult. The mountain of life has no top. Life is a continuous climb. There is no life of ease; no easy love relationship. You never get there. Sound hopeless? It is far from hopeless.

"You never get there" only means there is always something more to reach for; something past the looming precipice

How
To
Really
Love
the
One
You're
With!

LoveNote. . .

People seldom see the halting and painful steps by which the most insignificant success is achieved.
~ Annie Sullivan, Helen Keller's assistant.

that you cannot yet see. Relationships must be consistently worked on and you must not quit climbing. This perilous quest is never easy and it is always worthy of your best efforts.

At first it may seem that quitting is the answer. If you have ever tried quitting, you may have discovered that it is more difficult to go back down the mountain then to continue the climb for several reasons. First of all, going back down takes you back to where you were before you began. There's not much challenge in that.

The more steps you take in the right direction, the smarter you become about staying on the right path; the more skilled you become in developing strategies for the climb and the more you begin to enjoy the challenge of the adventure. As you continue to climb, so does your self-confidence. When you retreat, you lose ground; you have to start all over.

On your way up the mountain, you have already moved past some of life's most troublesome obstacles, so keep your eye on the target. Keep moving up. Unless you want to experience the same obstacles again in reverse order, keep climbing.

I suppose the question is: "Since you have a choice, which would you prefer: to return to where you started before you began the climb or to keep climbing with the one you love? When you run into an obstacle and when love is still present, should you quit or keep working on the relationship?"

Downhill is hard, too! The rewards of a continued climb far surpass the steps you may be tempted to take in the wrong direction.

"But the climb is too hard! I'm not sure how long I can continue."

It will be difficult if you continue and perhaps more diffi-

LoveNote. . .

In the mountains of truth, you never climb in vain. Either you already reach a higher point today, or you exercise your strength in order to be able to climb higher tomorrow.

~ Friedrich Nietzsche

LoveNote. . .

You cannot drift to the top of the mountain.

~ Jim Rohn

cult if you stop. You experience one set of circumstances when you move ahead and another set of circumstances when you quit. There is often pain in either choice. The choice that brings you the most pleasure may not always be the best choice. You must weigh the benefits of your choices. That is the way love relationships work. Love takes work. It takes lots and lots of work.

If you think that "someday" you will conquer the mountain; someday you will live "happily ever after," you are in for a big surprise. Someday is now! "Happily ever after" is the same as tomorrow - it never comes. This is it! Live happiness now.

That certainly does not mean you should give up. The climb is never easy. It takes consistent effort; a concept of team. Climbing as a team is a better idea. Working together is a must. There are no shortcuts to the top of a mountain that has no top.

If your love partner is not assisting the two of you in the climb, nothing you can do can change that. For them, changing is a personal decision. You cannot push a rope up the mountain. Keep climbing, alone if you must, but continue the climb. There is something new and exciting up there just for you, too! There are many important life and relationship lessons for you to discover on your quest for the summit.

Doesn't it make sense to push forward and continue to experience new and exciting things rather than continue to wallow in the past and be disappointed again by the same old stuff?

Although fear and risk may appear as obstacles to overcome along the way, the end result is a benefit worthy of accomplishment. I've had it with the past! Except to learn from, the past is useless. The future is now!

Your love relationship is either in a state of continual becoming - a steady, yet rugged climb to the top of the moun-

**How
To
Really
Love
the
One
You're
With!**

LoveNote. . .

It is a rough road that leads to the heights of success.

~ Seneca

LoveNote. . .

In love relationships, backward is not an option worthy of choice!

~ Larry James

tain; at a checkpoint, resting - a place where you take a breather, a place where you self-inquire, and where you take stock of the relationship together to determine what needs to be done to continue the climb, or your relationship is in a state of giving up - a place where you start back down the mountain, a task that may be more difficult than the climb itself.

Plot your course. Study the mountain.

Develop a team strategy. Team can conquer the mountain. The goal is a healthy love relationship anchored in unconditional love. The interesting thing is, you find love along the way. It is not something you must wait for. Love is now. It is your choice.

When love partners make a mutual decision to do what some might call an impossible thing, the chances of doing it more than double. Your energy is focused. The risk of failing decreases when you find solutions, make decisions together and get into action, or to coin a phrase, "continue the climb." All your energy is on the side of doing.

As you climb, occasionally find a ledge cozy enough for the two of you to rest, then re-create and celebrate love. Take time to celebrate your successes. Then, confidently re-group and begin climbing again.

Relationships are simple. Not easy. . . simple. Remember the "Golden Rule."

Uphill is hard.

Downhill is hard, too!

LoveNote. . .

You cannot keep the promise of a forever love relationship by yourself. You must honor the promise together. You cannot stand on the promise alone and really *be* together.

~ Larry James

LoveNote. . .

The ultimate meaning. . . of the promise I make today can be clear only at the end of my life; and the meaning of my life at its end will be different because I made this promise today.

~ Margaret Farley

LoveNote. . .

Honor your commitments.

~ Larry James

The Mutual Promise

♥

LARRY JAMES

A piece of paper cannot bind two hearts together. It is only the new beginning of a mutual promise. It takes love and diligent effort. It requires doing whatever it takes. You must have a mutual promise to support each other.

Commitment springs from the heart and is nurtured by compassion and understanding. The promise of love is a promise worthy of your best efforts. It deserves your highest level of commitment.

The promise of staying together comes from commitment; the kind of commitment that comes when you love someone unconditionally.

LoveNote. . .

Love is like quicksilver in the hand. Leave the fingers open and it stays. Clutch it, and it darts away.

~ Dorothy Parker

Let Go

♥

It may not be wise to become attached to what we think has to happen for our relationships to be great. Once we know what we want, consider simply letting it happen. This doesn't mean that we never have to do anything again. It only means that we let go of our attachments to what we think our relationships have to be to be great, and let them happen.

We often attach ourselves to outdated thoughts and ideas of how things should be. And we get disappointed a lot, and sometimes downright disgusted when the very concepts we hold onto turn on us in the middle of a love relationship that is supposed to be great.

Let go. Detach yourself from all of your "shoulds." Always do the very best you can and be clear that holding on to useless, old thoughts and ideas can only dis-empower your relationship, never enrich it.

On the other hand, for some, the natural thing to do is to look for the one idea that would make them feel great all the time. This is not a good idea. No one thing can make us feel great all the time. The concern is that our old self might be looking for another "good thing" we can become attached to or dependent upon.

What has to happen for a state of joy and happiness to be created in your love relationship over and over again so you can be happy and excited all the time and still get some work done? Let go of the past and always do the very best you can. Let go of what you used to do and who you used to be. From this point on, *always do the very best you can.*

A commitment to always do the best you can will never

How
To
Really
Love
the
One
You're
With!

LoveNote. . .

Detachment is not apathy or indifference. It is the pre-requisite for effective involvement. Often what we think is best for others is distorted by our attachment to our opinions: we want others to be happy in the way we think they should be happy. It is only when we want nothing for ourselves that we are able to see clearly into others' needs and understand how to serve them.

~ Mahatma Gandhi

allow feelings of guilt. When you are always doing the best you can, you have nothing to feel guilty about. You can never say, "I failed. If only I would have given it my best," because you know you did your best.

Let go of having the creation of a state of joy be a burden. Let go of thinking you know what has to be done to create a state of joy. There are far too many emotions, feelings and varying degrees of individual personalities for us to justify holding on to our own ideas of how a relationship has to be for us to be happy. You will never figure it out. Always doing the best you can, can be the state of joy and happiness you were looking for.

Acknowledge what you want, then be totally committed to doing whatever it takes to make it happen, and not be attached to what *you* think you must do to cause it to happen.

Follow your heart. Your heart only and always speaks Truth.

Being okay with the way relationships turn out is another way of saying it. Face it. On the surface, relationships seem to be unpredictable, however upon closer examination, they are often quite predictable. If you always do what you have always done, you will always get what you have always gotten.

"But life is such a struggle!"

"Oh? Is it really?"

Consider that if this is your belief. . . #1, it may be true, #2, it might not be true, or #3, it might be wise to reconsider that just because your parents or other people in your life seem to be destined to struggle, it doesn't mean you have to repeat this self-defeating behavior. It is not necessary for you to buy into this ridiculous idea. Consider that life is a struggle to only those who think that life has to be a struggle.

It may be a good idea for us to practice in a love relation-

**How
To
Really
Love
the
One
You're
With!**

LoveNote. . .

When you no longer need a relationship, then you are
ready to have a healthy one.

~ Karin Owen

LoveNote. . .

Marriage is a fragile relationship. *It does not take care of
you; you must take care of it.*

~ Larry Losoncy, Ph.D.

ship what a gardener practices in planting a flower seed. In the seed is the full manifestation of the flower in all its magnificence. The gardener doesn't have to make the seed grow. He never doubts that it will blossom into a beautiful flower. Other people's opinions do not interfere with his conviction that the seed of the flower contains within it everything necessary to create the beauty and fragrance of a flower. *He doesn't get lost in his attachment to the result.* He knows that it is there and all that is required is his attention and non-interference.

Let go of your attachments. Let them all go.

Let your relationships live themselves. Follow your heart.

Let go.

How
To
Really
Love
the
One
You're
With!

LoveNote. . .

Friends fantasize the future. Lovers embrace their
dream. Partners roll up their sleeves and get to work. It
takes all three - friend, partner, lover - to make this union.
Stretch, reach and claim what is yours together.

~ Warren Lane Molton

Invent Your Future Relationship

♥

LARRY JAMES

If you want to continually experience unconditional love in your relationship, you must invent how you would like for the relationship to be. If you are going to make it up, make it up the way you want it and communicate your newly-invented relationship model to your love partner. Share yourself. Be courageous and outrageous! Stretch.

Any construction of thought that moves you in the wrong direction is counter-productive. The only kind of "making it up" that serves you is the kind that moves you toward the kind of love relationship you want.

Whether you are in a committed relationship or looking for one, it is really possible to invent your future love relationship with the one you're with or the one you will be with, right now! The invention of a forever love relationship works best when it is a team effort.

If you only always expect your relationship to be like it was in the past, that is what you will get more of. Your past then, again becomes your future. It demonstrates your superior intelligence to work on guidelines for the kind of relationship you want and look for agreement from the one you're with, than to only hope for the best and accept what happens.

Invent a new and exciting love relationship; one you have never experienced before. Imagine the possibilities! An exciting love relationship filled with hot passion, unbridled love and romantic adventure is yours for the asking. If you don't invent it, you will always be wondering why nothing new and exciting ever happens in your relationship. Who has a greater interest in that than you? It is time to get to work.

How
To
Really
Love
the
One
You're
With!

LoveNote. . .

To achieve love which is lasting and truly satisfying, each of us must strive to cultivate love as a state of mind, and in giving love, we will receive it. Unconditional love knows no barriers and overcomes all difficulties. It is the only lesson we have to learn.

~ Eileen Campbell

An exciting, adventurous relationship only happens when you become exciting and adventurous!

With excitement and adventure present in your love relationship, you will never have to re-ignite the flame of love... only keep it burning.

To invent your own relationship is to be present to the moment, step into the future, and not allow yourself to drag the misery of past relationships with you. You deserve more than your past has to offer. Creation of your future is easier when you let go of the past. You can always move forward with greater ease and greater velocity when not carrying so much baggage.

When you invent something, you are literally creating something new. Invent a future healthy love relationship that is informed by the past, and is in no way shackled by its limitations.

Invent a relationship worthy of your undivided attention.

Many people will not allow themselves to even think about what they have not already experienced. It's not that they lack imagination, they just fail to put it into use. They tried it once and it didn't work, or they got hurt. It is scary. What if it doesn't happen? What if it doesn't work? How will I look? What if I get it, what will I do with it?

This is too scary! And the truth is, you just haven't experienced the future yet the way you have it made up and it sounds too good to be true. . . *and* scary. Nothing is too good to be true. Do I deserve it? Will it last? An unconditional love relationship has no room for fear in it.

To invent your own relationship is to create a new way of being in the relationship. . . one that empowers your relationship. . . one that empowers your love partner. Let go of how things have been and allow yourself to live a little. Let yourself experiment with some new thoughts of how you would like your relationship to be. Let yourself imagine

**How
To
Really
Love
the
One
You're
With!**

LoveNote. . .

An exciting, adventurous relationship only happens when you become exciting and adventurous! With excitement and adventure present in your love relationship, you will never have to re-ignite the flame of love. . . only keep it burning.

~ Larry James

LoveNote. . .

To define love is very difficult, for the same reason that words cannot fully describe the flavor of an orange. You have to taste the fruit to know its flavor. So with love.

~ Paramahansa Yogananda

LoveNote. . .

Love knows no pain.

~ Meister Eckhart

who you would have to become to have your relationship to be great.

The problem with most people is they cannot get past all of the "stuff" of past relationships. *A heart full of anger and resentment has no room for love.* People worry more about what they don't want. They live in fear of being alone again; of being abandoned.

Scratch those thoughts. Put them out of your mind. My friend, Joe Charbonneau says, "Of all the people who will never leave me, I am the only one!" There may be some comfort in that. You will never be alone as long as you have enough love for yourself for you to justify wanting to be with yourself. You can never be alone when you are with someone you love, even if it is yourself. You must get to this point before you can really *be* with someone else.

How would you like your relationship to be? Make it up that way!

Live in the present. Experience the empowering feeling of allowing yourself the freedom to be who you need to be in the future. . . right now. You have already experienced the past. If you want more of that, continue to focus on it and you will not be disappointed.

Create a future worth living into. In one of their brochures for "The Advanced Course," San Francisco based Landmark Education states, "When we are able to leave our past in the past and stand in the future, the possibilities for every aspect of our lives multiply exponentially."

Invent the miracle of a healthy love relationship anchored in unconditional love. Create together the ultimate expression of who you really are, when separate *and* together.

You are unconditional love. Share it. Joyously revel in it. Love is like rabbits. It multiplies. The more loving you are, the more people who are loving want to be around you.

LoveNote. . .

Let your bodies speak your truth. Make love with the consciousness that your body can say what you cannot, and know that in its sensuous abandon sexual passion is the dancing of the spirit!

~ Daphne Rose Kingma

LoveNote. . .

On with the dance – let joy be unconfined.

~ Mark Twain

The more love you have, the more there is to give away. Share it with your family of friends and relatives. Give it away to strangers. You will never run out.

Oh, yes. Something you must know by now. Unconditional love must be worked on every moment you are in a relationship with whoever you are giving it to. It is easier with strangers. Love to a stranger may be expressed by only a smile given in a passing moment. With a love partner it requires much more consistency of effort.

With a forever love partner you must also invent a forever commitment. You must use your imagination! You must always be present to the sense of something that is possible far beyond the ordinary. You must both be committed to whatever you decide that is. . . and express it to each other unconditionally.

Ah, love. What a wonderful adventure!

The Truth is. Love is always there. It has already been invented. Love invented itself. We must discover it. . . bring it to the surface. Then give it away. Never fear. As long as we have love for ourselves, we will never run out. We can only give away what we already have.

I love you.

**How
To
Really
Love
the
One
You're
With!**

LoveNote...

A marriage should be nurtured on high ideals and the wine of God's inspiration; then it will be a happy and mutually beneficial union.

~ Paramahansa Yogananda

Higher Communication II

♥

LARRY JAMES

Be thankful for your relationships.

All of them.

Seems to me that there may be only two prayers worthy of praying. One prayer is to know God. The other prayer is a prayer of thanksgiving.

Pray a prayer of self-discovery and one of gratitude, and know God is listening.

It is useless and wastes God's time and our mental energy to pray for things. God has given us the ability to choose. Our greatest power is choice. To use this power to choose to pray for things that God has already given us the power to create may not be an effective use of our time.

I can imagine God being amused. I can hear him saying, "Why don't they get it? I have given them everything and yet they insist upon asking me for the same things, over and over again."

It may not seem logical that we should only pray a prayer of thanksgiving. If we are someone who has always used our prayers for asking, this may sound strange to us. Strange, meaning different. This, to some, may appear to be an arrogant way to speak to God. Hardly.

God will view your prayers with greater reverence when you acknowledge that you have already been given the power to choose. Stop asking God to give you a great relationship. Instead, choose to thank God for a love relationship that transcends your own imagination, then do whatever you can to help it turn out that way.

233

**How
To
Really
Love
the
One
You're
With!**

LoveNote...

It doesn't hurt to pray for miracles, but I wouldn't waste much time on it. Save the prayers for thank-you's.

~ Allen Appel

LoveNote...

Love is the ultimate Truth at the heart of all creation.

~ Michael Jackson

In the past we have asked for a great relationship, never received it, and never bothered to do anything differently and wondered why God didn't answer our prayer. Hopefully, we have learned that lesson by now. That's like asking God for a great job and never going to look for one. Excuse me! I don't believe that's what God had in mind. We must be thankful *and* do something.

Being thankful is one of the keys to getting what you want. Cultivate the practice of affirmative prayer. An attitude of gratitude is faith in action. It is a very satisfying feeling to know that what you are thankful for, you will experience. What you focus on, manifests. Who you are is a good example of that.

Gratitude is the key that opens the door to everything you want in life. Saying a prayer of thanksgiving has you focus on the good things that are happening to you and the good things that are about to happen to you. That alone may be a good enough reason to only pray a prayer of thanksgiving. It creates a thirst for more of the good that God says is already yours. Think about it. You get what you really believe. God *always* answers prayer. There is great value in expecting your dreams to come true. . . and you must first be thankful and believe that they will.

I believe it may be okay to ask for something once in a while. It keeps God on His toes. It's okay, that is, if I remember I am only doing it to test God's good sense of humor.

Is it true that when something bad happens we tend to not want to take responsibility that the bad we see is what we created? Not taking responsibility means we try to find someone outside of ourselves to blame. When we ask God for things and the things don't come, who do we blame? When we blame God for not answering prayer, our love for God becomes conditional. There is no room for blame in an unconditional love relationship. For what good reason do we do this?

LoveNote...

Love is the spiritual force that girds us in our weak moments, heals us when nothing else can help, and gives us purpose. Not just to have life, but to live it fully and contentedly with love.

~ Joyce Hifler

LoveNote...

Real love only gives. It places no demands whatsoever and allows complete freedom. To love is to give all of yourself away to everyone at once, all the time, without any partiality, selectivity or variation. Rather than the ultimate sacrifice, this is the ultimate ecstasy. For like God, "you can give yourself completely, wholly without loss and only with gain."

~ A Course in Miracles

How can we justify loving Him conditionally when we, in our self-serving arrogance, resist believing that our misfortune is our own fault?

God *always* answers prayer. *Always*. It may not be the answer you want but he *always* answers.

Can we look at ourselves in the mirror, take complete responsibility for our relationships and all areas of our lives, and know that we do have choice and we do create our own reality? As within, so without. Consider saying 'yes' to prayers of self-discovery and thanksgiving and experience the miracle of good that God has already given to you.

Stop! Before you ask God for *things*, remember, you already have the power to create the things you want. Ernest Holmes said, "Change your thinking. Change your life!" Develop the habit of thanking God for the things He has given you the power to create. Then, get busy and do something.

Pray to know God or to thank God for His abundance.

Thank Him for being there for you. Be grateful for the gift of constant and faithful devotion He has given to help you get to know Him better. Let Him know how grateful you are for the relationships in your life. Offer thanks for your present circumstance, regardless of what you think or feel about it. Thank Him for the lessons of good you learn from the things you often call bad. Thank Him for the tears of joy and the tears of sadness.

Thank Him for more love, courage and understanding. Express gratitude for the everyday miracles that occur that you often take for granted. Be grateful for the power of choice. Thank God for creating the possibility of unconditional love and for the self-discipline to stay on that path. Thank Him for the opportunity to express gratitude. Be thankful for all that God has freely given.

Whatever you want in your relationships. . . wants you! Thank God for that, too!

How
To
Really
Love
the
One
You're
With!

LoveNote. . .

Sometimes we may find that our partner continues to seek satisfaction in ways that we cannot live with. Nevertheless, when we decide to go our own way we still have a choice as to how we separate. We can separate with bad feelings, blaming the other's faults and unacceptable behavior. Or we can separate with forgiveness, love and understanding.

~ Peter Russell

Who Would You Have to Become?

♥

LARRY JAMES

Once upon a time, I spent nearly sixteen months being with a wonderful woman whom I loved very much. I still do. I always will. Somehow there was a very special connection. *And* we are no longer together. I have discovered that it is possible to love someone and not be with them. It took me a while to be okay with that.

Separation, divorce or death do not end a relationship. . . they only change it. As long as you have memory you will always be related. We can recognize when a relationship is over *and* it never ends. The relationship only becomes different. . . *it never ends.*

Must separation put an end to friendship? Certainly not. Although we are apart, we remain friends. *And* that was a personal decision. We both acknowledge that the relationship can never again be as it was.

Even when people occasionally get back together, the relationship can only be different, never as it was. Sometimes better. Sometimes worse. Never as it was.

When we went our separate ways, I sought the assistance of a professional therapist. It was early during those nearly six months that it became very clear that I had very little idea about what I really wanted in a relationship.

In the past I had always accepted what showed up in a relationship and dealt with it as best I could. That was then. . . this is now. The old way of being in a relationship is no longer good enough for me. It is simply not acceptable.

During this period of self-discovery, I became more aware

**How
To
Really
Love
the
One
You're
With!**

LoveNote...

When you fail to hit the target, never in history has it been the target's fault.

~ Larry Winget

LoveNote...

With God nothing shall be impossible.

~ Luke 1:37

of who I was being that contributed to my relationship being over. I soon discovered my most pressing need. In my heart I felt a growing need to become deeply engrossed in a relentless search for who I would have to become to have a healthy love relationship.

Regardless of whether you are in a committed relationship or coming out of a relationship, relationships can always be better than they are. Do some careful analysis on *how* you can make things better. This is a strategy worthy of your very best efforts.

Who would *you* have to become to have your relationships be great? What could you do differently? Whose assistance could you request? How will you change? Or will you? Are you willing to stop trying to change your love partner?

It is not possible to change anyone else. Change is always a personal decision; an individual choice.

Communicate. . . with love. Be in constant communication about what you want and what you don't want. Demonstrate your commitment by pledging to help each other stay on the path of self-discovery and to always be opting for a love relationship anchored in unconditional love.

Then do something. . . together, as soon as you can and whenever you can.

Who would you have to become?

Think about it.

How
To
Really
Love
the
One
You're
With!

LoveNote. . .

The worst prison would be a closed heart.

~ Pope John Paul II

For Your Eyes Only

LARRY JAMES

♥

Have you ever sat down, discouraged and out of steam, stuck and with a sense of hopelessness about your relationship? Have you ever felt like you needed to express what you felt? Have you ever taken the opportunity to write some notes to yourself about how you are feeling; even the feelings you feel uncomfortable sharing with anyone? Do you feel a lack of freedom to fully express yourself?

I recommend writing a *"for your eyes only"* journal. Journaling creates a sense of freedom of expression. It is an excellent way to document your innermost thoughts and feelings of the moment.

"Why would I want to do that?"

One of the best ways to expedite release and healing is by keeping a daily journal. There are many other exciting possibilities to look forward to by journaling. It can truly be an adventure in self-discovery.

Buy a journal or hardbound notebook. They are available at most book stores or card and party shops. It is a book with blank pages. Then, begin to write. Write what happened, what you did, what your love partner did, how you felt and how you feel now, what you think, what your assessment of the situation is, what would have to happen for things to get better, and whatever comes into your mind. Write anything and everything.

Journaling is an opportunity to get down and dirty. Tell the truth from your perspective. And be clear that what you write is only your opinion of what happened. From where your love partner stands, there is always another opinion. Get it all out on paper where you can see it.

How
To
Really
Love
the
One
You're
With!

LoveNote. . .

Love becomes the ultimate answer to the ultimate human question.

~ Archibald Macleish

No one need read your journal but you. However, it could come in handy if you choose to enroll in therapy. To assist you best, your therapist needs to know everything relevant to why you chose therapy, what your issues are and more. A journal can be your ready reference about how you felt and how you are feeling now.

It is a time for self-honesty. Expressing your deepest feelings, in writing and in your own words, is good therapy. Journaling will help you get your thoughts and feelings out of your head so you can deal with them with your heart. It helps to make your thoughts tangible; it makes them more easily accessible to you for closer scrutiny. It is easier to deal with something you can see and touch.

I often review what I have written five or six months previously and discover that I no longer feel that way or I may think, "I can't believe I had such a hard time with that situation."

Journaling helps you keep track of your progress. It reveals hot spots; the areas in your relationship that need healing.

Give up writing to make yourself look good. Quit worrying about writing the *right* thing. Write whatever pops into your head and write it however it expresses itself on paper.

Remember, it is a time for self-honesty. Keep your integrity intact. You must keep your word with yourself before you can trust yourself to keep your word with someone else.

Sometimes the truth is ugly. If the truth hurts, maybe you should be grateful. At least it got your attention.

I have often found that what hurts the most or what I want to look at the least, is what I most need to handle first. I have learned that what you resist, persists.

Never use time as an excuse. This is important. Take time!

LoveNote...

It is not necessary to love everything about yourself to like who you are!

~ Karin Owen

LoveNote...

The differences between friends cannot but reinforce their friendship.

~ Mao Tse-tung

Keeping a daily journal contributes to you! Carry your journal with you. When a thought that you feel the need to express hits you, take a moment and write it down. You can always expound on it later.

Journaling is a healthy way of expressing yourself so you can get to know you better.

LARRY JAMES

LoveNote. . .

In the presence of hope. . . faith is born.   In the presence of faith. . . love becomes a possibility! In the presence of love. . . miracles happen!

~ Robert Schuller

. . . And If All Else Fails?

LARRY JAMES

♥

When you have done the best you can, and your relationship seems to be falling apart at the seams, what other possibilities exist? What can you do when you have difficulty sustaining intimacy in your relationship?

What options are available when the very foundation of trust is shaken by an indiscriminate act of infidelity? How can you fix things when one love partner outgrows the need for dependence and begins to noticeably relish the freedom that their new-found independence offers?

When you no longer feel exclusively special to each other; when you no longer feel recognized by the other or wanted or appreciated or perhaps you feel taken for granted, what can you do?

When the heart no longer beats faster in anticipation of the sexual intimacy you once shared, what then? How can you mend a broken heart?

Most people resist change until they are backed against the wall; until they feel that there is nothing else they can do.

Change takes courage. It means taking responsibility for your relationship and being brave enough to take that first step toward change while you are still afraid.

Change takes effort. You must do something different. Sometimes it is important to accept the fact that you may not be able to do it all by yourself or even with your love partner. If you need help, ask for it.

Love partnerships die of neglect. Money, sex, and family

How
To
Really
Love
the
One
You're
With!

LoveNote. . .

Love is essentially formless. It can neither be contained nor possessed. It is like a river. You can never put your foot in the same water twice - it is always flowing, continuously transforming.

~ Bob Mandel

problems are only symptoms, they are not the *cause*. If we value our relationships, we must learn that they require lots of love, attention to detail, time, dedication and continued maintenance.

The changes that are required to maintain an intimate and healthy love relationship are often bigger than both love partners can manage by themselves. When there is a desire to move through the rough spots that all love relationships inevitably experience; when love is present, and the desire for change is mutual, it is time to talk about working things out. . . together.

There are many ways to help us heal the hurt. Study after study has shown that when love partners have difficulties, first they consult their friends and relatives and the most common professional they approach is their medical doctor and in come cases, their spiritual leader.

It is unfortunate that many people often associate the seeking of the services of a professional marriage and family therapist as an admission of failure. So what? There is no shame in taking care of yourself. Therapy is one of the choices. It can make clear the way to see the light at the end of the tunnel.

So, you can now make a choice. To sit around, knowing there is a problem and not doing anything about it can be as painful as staying in an unhealthy love relationship because you are afraid of being alone again.

Studies say women are more likely to seek counseling than men. I am a man, so I can say this. *Sometimes men are jerks!* We often feel that we must maintain our ego-centered macho image by refusing to admit we may need help. What nonsense! Men are human beings, too. Human beings have problems. Some men often view seeking help as a weakness. What a crock!

To seek the advice of a professional when things are falling

**How
To
Really
Love
the
One
You're
With!**

LoveNote. . .

For your love relationship to be better, you must first want it to be better. Next, you must be brave enough to take positive steps in the direction the Truth tells you to be right.

~ Larry James

apart can only be a sign of strength. We use that same argument to justify why people should use our own professional services in our everyday work, yet we are too afraid or too stubborn to admit that *we* need help. We feel that we are "man enough" to work it out by ourselves.

Face it, men. We need help. All we can get!

We are afraid. We are afraid of what it will look like to our friends if they discover we are having relationship problems. We are men. We are supposed to be in control of things. Who says?

We are often more afraid of what people will think, than how much we value our relationship with the one we say we love. To me, that's stupidity in action.

We must first learn to acknowledge that we have a problem, then do whatever is consistent with our commitments to our relationship. A problem is anything that gets in the way of our commitments.

When you place a high value on your relationship; when you really love each other, seldom can any problem ever be too difficult to solve. Both love partners, however, must be willing to do whatever it takes. They must have a similar level of commitment to the recovery process.

To go to therapy or watch the slow, agonizing death of your relationship? That is the question. Successful relationships thrive on love. They do not self-correct. They must be worked on. Without love, your relationship weakens and dies.

When considering the option of therapy, some people are willing to put aside their preconceived notions about what works and what doesn't work. They love each other and can't seem to work things out by themselves so they finally come to the decision that to delay seeking assistance may cause irreparable damage to the relationship. That's smart!

**How
To
Really
Love
the
One
You're
With!**

LoveNote. . .

Things do not change; we change.

~ Henry David Thoreau

They make a choice to care less what others think and with unconditional love as their goal, focus on what must be done. They are able to break through their own self-imposed barriers and look for the opportunity that psychoanalysis and psychotherapy may offer.

Occasionally, self-discovery needs a boost. Therapists are excellent boosters. The good ones boost with questions that become guides to self-awareness, a commitment to personal integrity, self-confidence and overall self-discovery. Perhaps this is the very best way to become aware of what you didn't know you didn't know. This may be the number one reason to consider therapy. What do you have to lose? It may be a better choice than what you are now doing, which may be nothing, which as you know, isn't working!

So you have decided to go to therapy? Good decision. You must now decide to participate in therapy. Notice. I said participate. If you refuse to participate in therapy like you may have refused to fully participate in your relationship, you will find you will get the same results you now have in your relationship. Not fully participating does not work.

When you trust your heart, any decision you make to participate in therapy will be okay. Your heart only speaks the Truth. That's one less thing you have to worry about. Any decision you make with your heart will always be in your best interest. You can count on it!

You must learn to distinguish between head-talk and heart-talk. You will want to only heed the voice of the heart. Some call it intuition. Some call it the voice of God. Call it whatever you want. Only learn to recognize Its voice.

Refuse to listen to your head feeding you its varied menu of conversations of the past. They are designed to keep you somewhere in the past. Isn't that what you are now running from? The future love relationship you have dreamed about is before you and cannot be driven to advance itself by a daily diet of messages from the past.

**How
To
Really
Love
the
One
You're
With!**

LoveNote. . .

There can be no transforming of darkness into light and of apathy into movement without emotion.

~ Carl Jung

LoveNote. . .

The fire of love will not burn on alone. It must be watched carefully. If we are to keep the fire of love alive, we must do whatever is necessary to keep the flames replenished whatever the cost. Love's fire feeds off the energy we put into keeping it burning!

~ Larry James

It is my opinion that you can best be served by going to therapy for questions, not answers. *And* it is only my opinion.

Other forms of therapy also have redeeming value and work equally as well in most cases. However, 'what's good for the goose is good for the gander' may not always be the truth. Different strokes were invented for different folks.

The answer is most often found in the question. A good therapist will ask many questions. Until you are ready to make some changes you may not be ready to deal with what you know needs to be done. It may also be difficult to understand that you already know the answers.

When you are in the midst of worry, pain and the fear of separation, it is tough to focus on the answers you already know. You allow fear to keep you from mustering up the courage necessary to face the truth of what must be done. The carefully designed questions of a skilled therapist can assist you in uncovering the answers you didn't know you knew.

When you discover answers to a therapist's questions given from a professional perspective and your answers are grounded in a commitment to personal integrity, you experience a sense of personal achievement and a feeling of self-confidence. You have experienced a breakthrough of the heart! It's that voice we were talking about earlier.

Go to therapy together. . . hand in hand. Put aside your differences in favor of a future together, anchored in unconditional love. Therapy works best when love partners who are searching for solutions to their difficulties and are willing to support each other in the process, see the therapist together. It is a demonstration of love and support for each other that is recommended and needed.

When you go to therapy only to appease your love partner or when you view therapy as a waste of time or just another

How
To
Really
Love
the
One
You're
With!

LoveNote...

We are what and where we are because we have first imagined it.

~ Donald Curtis

LoveNote...

Where there is no vision, the people perish.

~ Proverbs 29:18

LoveNote...

Some day after we have mastered the winds, the waves, the tides and gravity, we will harness for God the energies of love, and then, for the second time in the history of the world, people will have discovered fire.

~ Teilhard de Chardin

phase in the relationship that will pass with time, you may be wasting your time and your money. It's like taking a step in the right direction for all the wrong reasons. You are only fooling yourself.

Further, you may find that your lover will choose therapy in spite of you. They may discover the answers they were looking for. Because of your resistance to self-discovery you may feel left out in the cold. You may find yourself out-distanced by your love partner's own personal recovery and may experience the feeling of being left behind. The danger of actually being left behind could become a reality.

If, for any reason, going to therapy together is not possible, begin the journey alone. It is far better to be on this path alone, than to hold back because your lover refuses to go, and as a result, you delay making a connection with the information that could assist you in the healing of an often painful and unhealthy relationship. Making you your number one priority in this scenario is a healthy choice.

Therapy and writing have assisted me in working through the denial, loneliness, guilt, rejection, grief and anger. I highly recommend Bruce Fisher's book, *"Rebuilding When Your Relationship Ends,"* to assist in this process. Many more wonderful books to assist you in having healthy relationships can be found in the section, "LoveBooks and More!", on page 273 of this book.

Stepping into the therapy arena must be done with love and an attitude of expectancy for positive results. Having an open mind is a good idea. When you love someone and have a desire to work things out, it is essential to put your ego aside and do what must be done.

Therapists are trained to assist you in moving beyond the anger, resentment and criticism to acceptance, forgiveness, understanding and the fulfillment of mutual needs. Therapists have no magic answers, only helpful questions and a few suggestions offered as possibilities for choices. They

LoveNote...

Take away the cause, and the effect ceases.

~ Miguel De Cervantes

LoveNote...

You are only lonely when you don't like the person you are alone with.

~ Wayne Dyer

can assist you by asking questions that lead you to discover your own answers that point out how these needs can mutually be met.

In therapy, a wise counselor will not take sides with either love partner. They are not there to judge or give advice, but rather to help identify the problems and initiate an inquiry that both sides can participate in to reach their own healthy conclusions.

Therapy can effectively move you through the paralysis that problems with money, sex, family issues and many other issues cause in a relationship when you let them. You will be encouraged to listen to what your love partner has to say; *to really listen.* This is not a time to continue *arguing about*; it is a time to *listen for* what's missing in the relationship.

Obviously, both love partners have differing opinions. Part of the therapist's task is to help you find the common ground from which you both can begin to rebuild or repair your love relationship. Both love partners must be motivated to preserve the relationship.

Enrolling in therapy to seek questions re-enrolls you in your love relationship. It requires getting back to the basics. You get active in the relationship with yourself. You become excited about what you are learning about you and who you are becoming. For me, this style of therapy suggests that we already know what must be done and we have but to discover this Truth through individual inquiry. A skilled therapist can assist you in getting to the heart of the matter. I value this lofty ideal for the Truth it is. It will always set you free. . . often in more ways than one.

Therapy promotes lasting personal development. You remember most and cherish most dearly that which you discover on your own. You begin to see some possibilities. You discover a zest for living. You become excited about life once again! Therapy is truly an adventure in self-dis-

LoveNote. . .

Conflict and love: do they go together? Absolutely! Do most couples realize that conflict is an opportunity to help their love grow? No, they do not. Your conflict *can* be loving and productive, and both of you can win.

~ Larry Losoncy, Ph.D.

covery. Achieving this state takes diligent effort, a commitment to be your best and a strong belief in the benefits of the desired results, both to you and to your love partner.

You feel the need to share your personal discovery with anyone who will listen. . . perhaps even your love partner. Isn't that a novel idea? It's like giving away love as fast as you receive it. What you give has a profound effect on what you receive.

Putting more love into the relationship, in most cases, will create more love in return. Love is the answer to all questions. I have discovered that my universe works best when I acknowledge and am grateful for the Truth of this Divine idea.

Egos aside, a common excuse for not going to a professional therapist is money. Some insurance policies will cover part, if not all, of your investment in therapy. If you have no insurance, find a way! Therapy doesn't cost. . . it pays. To obtain the rewards of therapy may require sacrifice. Giving up something in favor of having your relationship work demonstrates your commitment to it.

Healing and growth take time. Remember, infants want things now. Mature love partners can wait. Building healthy love relationships is a never-ending process. Don't rush things. Patience is required.

Another thought. Often counseling is considered as a last resort. After talking with friends, relatives, a medical doctor or spiritual leader, and sometimes anyone who will listen, many often feel they are at the end of the proverbial rope. There is nowhere to turn. They come to therapy after exhausting all hope.

In some cases they come to therapy to validate their own idea that they truly may be incompatible. The unfortunate thing is, if you wait until you reach this point, it could be too late. It is rarely too late if the commitment to spiritual and personal growth is present.

LoveNote. . .

So long as two individuals live together they will have differences. You and your mate will be in conflict for as long as you are mates. You have no choice about conflict: it *will* occur. Your choices have to do with what kind of conflict you will have. What will it be; win-lose? lose-win? lose-lose? or win-win?

~ Larry Losoncy, Ph.D.

LoveNote. . .

To stick with a mistake is worse than making one.

~ Malcolm Forbes

Preventative maintenance is also a good idea. This can serve as a wonderful tool for supporting love partners in a healthy love relationship. It is wise to review and assess your relationship at regular intervals.

Attend workshops and seminars. Read books designed to have love partners working together to foster the restoration of integrity in love relationships, unconditional love, better understanding, forgiveness, acceptance and all of the values we cherish as part of a healthy love relationship. We must consistently work together to *change* our past behavior.

Where do you go for good therapy? My suggestion is to call your local Mental Health Association. They can offer referrals based upon your needs and ability to pay. Now, now, be careful that you don't become turned off by the words mental health. The truth is, everyone is a little crazy anyway! We are all crazy about different things at different levels.

Acknowledge your responsibility in the matter and be wise; stretch yourself. Seek assistance. Now is the time to put aside what *you* think and do something. Every love relationship has difficulties at various levels. That's right. Every relationship.

Men and women are different. With so many variables in a relationship, it is a wonder that men and women get along as well as they do.

So, if you want to work things out, dump your preconceived ideas about what people will think or what your love partner will think if you choose to pursue therapy on your own. They are going to think whatever they think and there isn't anything that you can do about it. Besides, it doesn't matter what they think. It's your problem. You must do what you must do. At least, you will be taking a brave step forward; a step that, with time, can dissolve the obstacles that are currently preventing you from the healthy love relationship you so richly deserve.

Just do it!

**How
To
Really
Love
the
One
You're
With!**

LoveNote. . .

When you nurture, you're compassionate. That means listening, holding, comforting, caring, doing for. That means the touch and the gesture which say you care. That means asking how your mate is feeling or doing, and then listening for the answer. To have a happier, healthier marriage, communicate love and support to your mate daily.

~ Larry Losoncy, Ph. D.

Love Chart

Mark Victor Hansen

I am love!
I am loving, loved and beloved.
I give and receive abundant love.
I see love everywhere in everything.
I feel love. . . right here and right now.
I speak only with love in my heart.
I desire and deserve love.
I am a love magnet.
Love serves me and I serve love.
I am the self-generator of love.
With my love I create
Beauty, truth, health, and happiness,
Success, prosperity and more love.
I live in love
More fully each day.

LoveNote. . .

"Come on, Mom and Dad! Wake up!" she said as she tugged at the bedspread. "It's morning! See the sun? The day is full of *love* and the sky is full of birds and stuff!"

~ Kelly Jarvis, Age 2 ½
The Author's Daughter

Nineteen years later. . .

LoveNote. . .

"A wake-up call from an angel! Her words coaxed me from slumber in a memorable way. What a wonderful way to begin a lazy Sunday morning. I remember it well. I love you, Kelly!"

~ Larry James, Age 54
Kelly's Dad

LoveNote. . .

The miracle of unconditional love is nurtured by the power of the Divine and our own imagination. *Imagine the possibilities!*

~ Larry James

How
To
Really
Love
the
One
You're
With!

LoveNote...

Forgiveness, with love, is an absolute necessity for the successful demonstration of prosperity.

~ James Melton

HindSight!

In my life, there have been many excellent teachers who have fostered understanding and creativity and who have planted the seeds of intellectual curiosity that will grow and blossom within me for the rest of my life. For this, I am thankful. I have read hundreds of books and attended many seminars and workshops on many subjects and have been enlightened by them all.

Within the pages of this book you may find some of the words and phrases to be familiar. While writing Part One, I found it useful to incorporate some of their carefully distilled ideas with words of my own. I have discovered that they have become so entangled with my own words that I am no longer able to distinguish their origin to offer the credit their authors so richly deserve. I have given my best to the effort of acknowledging them where memory serves me. I ask forgiveness from all others.

Many of their books are recommended reading and can be found in the section, "LoveBooks and More!"

How
To
Really
Love
the
One
You're
With!

LoveNote...

The true university of these days is a collection of books.

~ Carlyle

LoveNote...

If a man empties his purse into his head, no one can take it away from him. An investment in knowledge always pays the best interest.

~ Benjamin Franklin

LoveNote...

Some books are to be tasted, others to be swallowed, and some few to be chewed and digested.

~ Francis Bacon

LoveNote...

The man who doesn't read good books has no advantage over the man who can't read them.

~ Mark Twain

LoveBooks and More!

Recommended Reading, Listening and Viewing

LARRY JAMES

♥

If you are intent on having a truly incredible love relationship, you must always remember that you must consistently continue to work on it. Never take your love relationship or your love partner for granted. If you do, you can confidently expect your love relationship to slowly disintegrate into nothingness. I have found that reading in an area that needs improvement always lends a certain amount of assistance not ordinarily found in everyday living and loving.

The books listed on the following pages have been a tremendous help to me in my search for guidelines that foster a healthy love relationship. Always read with an open mind! Look for new ideas. If a new thought is contrary to your current belief system, never, on first reading, reject it. Think about it. Ponder on it. Write it down, look at it for several days. See if it might work for you. If it works, great. If not, toss it and move on.

Be your own critic. Rarely accept other people's opinions about books. Read them and rate them for yourself. Their opinion is only their opinion. Generally speaking, it only relates to who they are in their own situation. . . seldom, if ever can someone else's opinion clearly relate to your very own personal situation. Make your own decisions.

Be coachable when you are reading. Be open for new and exciting ideas that can put the fire back in your love relationship or can open up all kinds of new possibilities for future love relationships.

Readers are people who have a commitment to mutual growth; to become the best they can be, first for themselves

**How
To
Really
Love
the
One
You're
With!**

LoveNote. . .

Drink deeply from good books.

~ John Wooden

LoveNote. . .

Man's mind stretched to a new idea never goes back to its original dimensions.

~ Oliver Wendell Holmes

LoveNote. . .

A book is the precious lifeblood of a master spirit.

~ John Milton

LoveNote. . .

Books are nourishment to the mind.

~ Italian Proverb

LoveNote. . .

I love good books. They inspire. They stimulate my thinking and challenge me to be the best I can be. Books offer encouragement; they assist me in being on the path of self-discovery.

~ Larry James

and second, for their love partner. Be a reader! Read the same books together. Share workable ideas openly. Mutually agree to commit to work on them together.

I recommend that you read for at least fifteen minutes before you go to bed each evening. Put some good stuff in your head before you retire. It will greatly enhance the level of comfort you attain while going to sleep. It will also help you to put aside the troubles of the day and help you concentrate on the good stuff you will want to think about and dream about. Your mind can then work on what needs to be worked on at a subconscious level while you are asleep.

When you read for fifteen minutes each day, you can complete a minimum of 18 average-sized books each year. Think about it! Do you think that reading and gaining the information available from 18 books can transform your love relationship? The answer is, "perhaps."

It is wise to remember that knowing something does not make a difference. Action is required! When you put to use the information you acquire from reading 18 books each year, I guarantee that your relationships and your life will work better. Go ahead. Try it! What have you got to lose? What if it works?

~ ~ ~

The Bible

A Course in Miracles. Glen Elen, CA: Foundation for Inner Peace, 1992.

Andrews, Frank. **The Art and Practice of Loving: 144 Ways to Enrich Your Experience of Love.** NY: Putman Publishing Group, 1992.

Beattie, Melody. **Codependent No More.** San Francisco: Harper, 1987.

**How
To
Really
Love
the
One
You're
With!**

Bloomfield, M.D., Harold H. **Love Secrets for a Lasting Relationship.** New York: Bantam Books, 1992.

Boe, Anne. **How to Net Your Playmate!** (Video) Encinitas, CA: Career Networks, 1993.

Bradshaw, John. **Homecoming.** NY: Bantam Books, 1990.

Buscaglia, Leo F. **Living, Loving and Learning.** NY: Ballantine, 1982.

Buscaglia, Leo F. **Loving Each Other.** (Audio Cassettes) Chicago: Nightingale-Conant, 1992.

DeAngelis, Ph.D., Barbara. **How to Make Love All the Time.** NY: Dell Publishing, 1987.

Dominian, Jack. **Dynamics of Marriage.** Mystic, CT: Twenty-Third Publications, 1993.

Dyer, Dr. Wayne W. **Your Erroneous Zones.** NY: Avon Books, 1976.

Ferrini, Paul. **The Twelve Steps of Forgiveness.** Santa Fe, NM: Heartways Press, 1991.

Findley, Guy. **The Secret of Letting Go.** St. Paul, MN: Llewellyn Publications, 1990.

Fisher, Ed.D., Bruce. **Rebuilding When Your Relationship Ends.** San Luis Obispo, CA: Impact Publishers, 2nd Edition, 1992.

Fisher, Ed.D., Bruce and Hart, Nina. **Reconnecting With Myself and Others.** San Luis Obispo, CA: Impact Publishers, 1994.

Fromm, Erich. **The Art of Loving.** NY: Harper & Row, 1956.

Godek, Gregory J. P. **1001 Ways to Be Romantic.** Weymouth, MA: Casablanca Press, 1993.

Godek, Gregory J. P. **1001 More Ways to Be Romantic.** Weymouth, MA: Casablanca Press, 1993.

Goldberg, Herb. **The Hazard of Being Male.** NY: Signal, 1976.

Gould, Roger. **Transformations.** NY: Simon & Schuster, 1978.

Hafen, Brent Q. & Frandsen, Kathryn J. **People Need People.** Evergreen, CO: Cordillera Press, Inc., 1987.

Hay, Louise L. **You Can Heal Your Life.** Carson, CA: Hay House, Inc., 1984.

Hendrix, Ph.D., Harville. **Getting The Love You Want: A Guide for Couples.** NY: Harper & Row, 1988.

Hendrix, Ph.D., Harville. **Keeping the Love You Find: A Guide for Singles.** NY: Pocket Books, 1992.

Hill, Napoleon. **Think and Grow Rich.** NY: Fawcett, 1979.

Hill, Napoleon. **Grow Rich With Peace of Mind.** Greenwich, CT: Fawcett Publications, 1967.

James, John W. and Cherry, Frank. **The Grief Recovery Handbook: A Step-by-Step Program for Moving Beyond Loss.** NY: Harper & Row, 1988.

James, Larry. **The First Book of Life$kills: 10 Ways to Maximize Your Personal & Professional Potential!** Tulsa, OK: Career Assurance Press, 1992.

Jampolsky, M.D., Gerald G. **Love is Letting Go of Fear.** Berkeley, CA: Celestial Arts, 1979.

Jampolsky, M.D., Gerald G. & Cirincione, Diane V. **Creating Positive Relationships.** (Audio Cassettes) Chicago: Nightingale-Conant, 1993.

Jampolsky, M.D., Gerald G. & Cirincione, Diane V. **Finding the Miracle of Love in Your Life.** (Audio Cassettes) NY: Bantam Audio Publishing, 1989.

Jeffers, Ph.D., Susan. **The Journey from Lost to Found.** NY: Ballantine Books, 1993.

Johnson, M.D., Spencer. **The One Minute Father.** NY: William Morrow, 1983.

Johnson, M.D., Spencer. **The One Minute Mother.** NY: William Morrow, 1983.

Kohe, J. Martin. **Your Greatest Power.** Chicago: Success Unlimited, 1953.

Levinson, Daniel. **Seasons of a Man's Life.** NY: Ballantine Books, 1978.

Losoncy, Ph.D., Larry. **What God Has Joined Together.** Tulsa, OK: Virgil W. Hensley, Inc., 1986.

Lynberg, Michael. **The Gift of Giving.** NY: Ballantine Books, 1991.

Mandino, Og. **The Greatest Miracle in the World.** NY: Frederick Fell Publishers, 1975.

McGinnis, Alan Loy. **The Friendship Factor.** Minneapolis: Augsburg Publishing House, 1979.

McGinnis, Alan Loy. **The Romance Factor.** NY: HarperCollins, 1982.

Merton, Thomas. **No Man is an Island.** NY: Harcourt Brace Jovanovich, 1978.

Nelson, Gertrude Mueller. **Here All Dwell Free: Stories to Heal the Wounded Feminine.** NY: Doubleday, 1991.

Owen, LCSW, CADC, Karin. **Relationship With Self.** Tulsa, OK: Discovery Books, 1992.

Paul, Ph.D., Margaret & Jordan. **Do I Have to Give Up Me to Be Loved By You?** Minneapolis: CompCare Publications, 1983.

Peale, Norman Vincent. **The Power of Positive Thinking.** Englewood Cliffs, NJ: Prentice-Hall, 1954. NY: Fawcett, 1978.

Peck, M.D., M. Scott. **The Road Less Traveled.** NY: Simon & Schuster, 1978.

Perry, Robert. **Special Relationships: Illusions of Love.** West Sedona, AZ: Robert Perry, 1992.

Peterson, Sylvia Ogden. **From Love That Hurts to Love That's Real: A Recovery Workbook.** NY: Prentice Hall/ Parkside, 1989.

Ponder, Catherine. **Pray and Grow Rich.** West Nyack, New York: Parker Publishing Company, 1968.

Prather, Hugh. **Notes to Myself.** NY: Bantam Books, 1970.

Rilke, Rainer Maria. **Letters to a Young Poet.** NY: Norton, 1993.

Shinn, Florence Scovel. **The Game of Life.** NY: Simon & Schuster, Inc., 1986.

Viorst, Judy. **Necessary Loses.** NY: Ballantine, 1986.

Viscott, M.D., David. **The Language of Feelings.** NY: Simon & Schuster, 1976.

How
To
Really
Love
the
One
You're
With!

Waller, Robert James. **The Bridges of Madison County.** NY: Warner Books, 1992.

Watson, Lillian Eichier. **Light From Many Lamps.** NY: Simon & Schuster, 1951.

Welwood, John. **Journey of the Heart: Intimate Relationships and the Path of Love.** NY: HarperCollins, 1990.

Williamson, Marianne. **A Return to Love: Reflections on the Principles of 'A Course in Miracles'.** NY: HarperCollins Publishers, 1992.

Wright, H. Norman. **Seasons of a Marriage.** Ventura, CA: Regal Press, 1982.

About Larry James. . .

Larry James is founder and President of Career Assurance Network. He was a popular Midwest radio personality in the 1960's and early 1970's.

He has earned his reputation as a speaker and workshop leader by teaching success principles and techniques he has learned and developed from his own experiences.

He fully acknowledges his responsibility to practice what he teaches; inspiring others by example.

His purpose is *"Helping others help themselves."* He is a student of Truth and is totally committed to sharing ideas and information that will improve communications in personal and business relationships. He has authored several books and audio cassette programs to assist in that process.

His **"Relationship Enrichment LoveShop,"** adapted from his best selling books, **"How to *Really* Love the One You're With: Affirmative Guidelines for a Healthy Love Relationship"** and **"LoveNotes for Lovers: Words That Make Music for Two Hearts Dancing"** is presented nationally and is designed to help people fit the pieces of the relationship puzzle together in a healthy way. A story of love written to honor the memory of his mother appears in the New York Times #1 Best Selling Book, **"A 2nd Helping of Chicken Soup for the Soul"** by Mark Victor Hansen and Jack Canfield.

He is also on staff with Dr. John Gray, Ph.D. author of **"Men Are From Mars, Women Are From Venus,"** and was Dr. Gray's personal choice to host the popular "Mars & Venus Chat Room" on America Online (Keyword: Mars).

Larry has appeared on hundreds of radio talk shows. His articles have appeared in numerous magazines nationwide. He is a member of National Speakers Association and is listed in **"Who's Who In Professional Speaking!"** He travels nationally leading seminars and giving speeches of inspiration that focus on developing close personal and business relationships. He champions the value of networking and has been called the *"Guru of Networking!"*

**How
To
Really
Love
the
One
You're
With!**

About Career Assurance Network. . .

Career Assurance Network is a company specializing in the presentation of "Relationship Enrichment LoveShops," business relationship development seminars and keynotes.

Career Assurance Network, whose acronym is *CAN*, is committed to providing services and products that will assist you in being *the best you CAN be!* Larry's books and audio learning systems are available from the publishing arm of our network, Career Assurance Press (CAPress1@aol.com).

About Life$kills Learning Systems. . .

A complete list of Larry's audio learning systems, books and other products designed to help you be the best you can be is available upon request.

If you are interested in a list of available seminar or keynote topics or in contacting Larry to arrange a personal appearance, please write to the address below or call our toll-free number.

Larry James would love to hear from you!

If this book, or any other work of the author has made a difference in your life or if you have ideas you would like to contribute, please take a moment and let him know. Send all correspondence to the address below.

Larry James
CAREER ASSURANCE NETWORK
Post Office Box 12695